BITING THE HAND THAT FEEDS THEM

Biting the Hand
That
Feeds Them

ORGANIZING WOMEN ON WELFARE AT THE GRASS ROOTS LEVEL

Jacqueline Pope

PRAEGER

New York
Westport, Connecticut
London

Library of Congress Cataloging-in-Publication Data

Pope, Jacqueline.
  Biting the hand that feeds them : organizing women on welfare
at the grass roots level / Jacqueline Pope.
    p.   cm.
  Bibliography : p.
  Includes index.
  ISBN 0-275-92922-1 (alk. paper)
    1. Welfare rights movement—New York (N.Y.)—History. 2. Poor
women—New York (N.Y.)—History. 3. Welfare recipients—New York
(N.Y.)—History. 4. Brooklyn (New York, N.Y.) I. Title.
  HV99.N59P66 1989
  362.8'3'097471—dc19   88-27505

Library of Congress Catalog Card Number: 88-27505
ISBN: 0-275-92922-1

First published in 1989

Praeger Publishers, One Madison Avenue, New York, NY 10010
A division of Greenwood Press, Inc.

Printed in the United States of America

The paper used in this book complies with the
Permanent Paper Standard issued by the National
Information Standards Organization (Z39.48-1984).

10 9 8 7 6 5 4 3 2 1

Contents

Preface

The Brooklyn Welfare Action Council (B-WAC) was a grass roots cooperative established in 1967 by women of color (ages 27–55) who received public assistance. Its purpose was to obtain social and economic benefits for its members through the promotion of changes within the system. By the time B-WAC disbanded in 1973, it had achieved the development of indigenous leaders who could preside over community institutions founded during the years of its existence.

As members of a nationwide effort — the National Welfare Rights Organization (NWRO) — activists labored to solidify the dignity of and to secure some measure of power for people on society's economic bottom. However, the Brooklyn contingent distinguished itself by being the sole welfare rights group that was controlled by and addressed the needs of welfare recipients.

METHODOLOGY

Employing a historical approach, I chronicled the welfare recipients' activities, analyzed their strategies, and examined B-WAC's weaknesses and strengths. Personal interviews figured prominently in the research. A total of 39 former

B-WAC members including 21 former organizers, as well as city officials, Welfare Department staff, and Brooklyn civil rights activists were questioned about their experiences with B-WAC during those years. B-WAC's first chairperson, Joyce Burson, was available for several interviews. She further assisted me by contacting former leaders and organizers for interviews.

Joyce Burson also allowed me access to her personal records. Additionally, brochures, newsletters, newspapers, minutes, articles, activists' correspondence, pictures, reports, B-WAC administrative files, monographs, scholarly journals, magazines, and welfare department documents relating to the welfare rights era, in addition to materials in the possession of organizers, were compiled and examined. Finally, current activists were interviewed concerning — among other issues — theories on motivation and the impact of 1960s actions on the problems faced by needy people in the 1980s.

Personal observations will be included because of my extensive involvement in the welfare rights movement during pre– and post–B-WAC days. When B-WAC was established, I was on public assistance; I became its first volunteer public relations director, the editor of its newsletter, and a training instructor. In 1969, I left B-WAC to assume the dual position of editor and assistant training director at the National Welfare Rights Organization office in Washington, D.C. Any distortion of the analysis and objectivity in this volume stemming from those activities and partisanship must be judged by the reader.[1]

Some questions to be addressed here are:

- What factors motivated the women to organize and strive for a more equitable society?
- Did their collective efforts affect social attitudes or national urban and welfare policies?
- Is it organization or mobilization that is the approach most likely to advance positive social change for low- and grant-income people?

— What role did religion and class play in their organizing efforts?

— What were the strengths and weaknesses of B-WAC?

— Can urban social planners design programs that encourage grass roots leadership and human development by adopting the strategies that B-WAC participants used?

In this study, planning is defined as a process in which one strives for clearly identified goals, priorities, and options, and predicts their consequences; it involves a continual monitoring, evaluation, and feedback regarding strategy and programs. Alfred Kahn, in Theory and Practice of Social Planning, sums up planning theory in one sentence: "Planning is a policy choice and programming in the light of facts, projections and applications of values."[2] Planning's immutable strengths are its interdisciplinary aspects or foci. In that light, this research endeavors to enhance public policy analysis and development by establishing a common or shared foundation on which urban social planners and other social scientists can design or foster political and social environments that are equitable for all Americans — especially the disenfranchised. Finally, the study will reveal fresh knowledge of poor women's social change activities, and shed light on human development issues, as well as promote additional research on this movement.

NOTES

1. Faced with the same circumstances, Richard Cloward and Frances Fox Piven made a similar comment in *Poor People's Movements: Why They Succeed — How They Fail* (New York: Vintage Books, 1979), p. 266.

2. Alfred Kahn, *Theory and Practice of Social Planning* (New York: Russell Sage Foundation, 1969), p. 17.

Acknowledgments

My sincere appreciation to Stockton State College, Pomona, New Jersey, for making this book possible through its generous funding, including the Distinguished Fellowship award.

Also special mention must be made of the assistance, patience, and complete faith of my daughters, Nneka, Donna, Rhonda, and Laurie; my mother, Elizabeth Cotmon; and my best friend, Joyce Burson. I am grateful to Sandra Moore, who typed numerous drafts without complaint. My appreciation is extended to Richard Maize, whose support for this effort began in undergraduate school; and to the former nuns and priests who organized in Brooklyn. The initial assistance of Professors Elizabeth Higgenbotham (Memphis State University) and Muruku Waiguchu (Paterson College) cleared the way for this book.

Finally, to all the courageous multitalented heroines raising their families alone and still fighting the "Department," I salute you. This is just one aspect of our story, because the real struggle continues.

Forward ever, backward never.

BITING THE HAND
THAT
FEEDS THEM

1

The Background

Historically, the goal of the poor — along with everyone else — has been to improve their status in society. In concert with middle- and high-income people, they have created national and local movements to further this goal. The 1960s were distinguished by the birth or expansion of several such movements — among them the struggle for human and civil rights. Presumably, people receiving public assistance were active in many of these struggles, but they did not typically identify themselves as welfare recipients. It is likely that these women and men were ashamed of their situation, and so their participation went unrecorded. However, this posture changed between 1963 and 1973, when people receiving public assistance acknowledged their low economic status and established the National Welfare Rights Organization (NWRO), with members throughout the United States, Canada, and Sweden.

In New York City, the Brooklyn Welfare Action Council (B-WAC)[1] was the largest and most important of the many protest groups that emerged in the metropolis during this turbulent period. A vehicle for improving the quality of life for its members, B-WAC was successful in some ways and at least effective in others. This is a study of the B-WAC organization, strategy, and membership. Furthermore, it documents and

examines the strengths and weaknesses of B-WAC and deter-
mines whether social planners can employ grass roots
strategies to meet and advance the concerns of grant-income
people. It investigates the motivation of activists and their
struggle to gain support from other welfare recipients, from the
working poor, from the middle class, and from political leaders.

B-WAC was the largest organization of its kind in the country.
It was established in 1967 by middle-aged women of color for the
purpose of obtaining social and economic benefits for members
and promoting changes in the welfare system. It had the strength
to mobilize thousands of public assistance clients in 1968, claiming
8,000 participants – or 40 percent of the national membership of
NWRO.[2] B-WAC fostered numerous social changes through
events that had a positive impact on the lives of all people receiving
welfare grants in the borough. Among these occurrences was the
citywide release of $41,590,788 directly to poor people in 1968 –
nearly a 3,000 percent increase from 1963 (see Table 1.1).[3] These
one-time grants had been withheld by local Welfare Department
officials, some of whom did not know that the clients were entitled
to the funds. Additionally, B-WAC and other welfare rights groups
around the nation turned the question of a national financial
support system into a public issue.

B-WAC's (and other groups') lobbying, organizing, and street
demonstrations in the fall of 1970 may have prompted the legislation for a national Family Assistance Plan (FAP) that was drafted
and submitted to Congress by the Nixon administration. Unfortunately, welfare rights members were unable to endorse this
legislation because the proposed allowance was too low. Politically
conservative Americans were also opposed to the bill, regarding
it as perilously close to socialism. Amazingly, these two politically
opposed groups were – for the first time – on the same side of an
issue. The measure was defeated in 1972.

Nonetheless, welfare rights members continued their activism,
and acquired valuable political knowledge and enhanced self-confidence. Their organizing activities increased as the shame and
guilt associated with poverty declined.

Table 1.1
Aid to Dependent Children
Special One-time Grants*

| | 1963 | | |
	Citywide	Brooklyn	Manhattan
June	$ 264,604	$142,759	$101,231
July	501,929	166,335	270,215
August	471,652	171,110	151,040
Totals	$1,238,185	$480,204	$522,486
Percent Increase 1963 & 1968	3,259	2,598	1,851

| | 1968 | | |
	Citywide	Brooklyn	Manhattan
June	$14,074,425	$ 3,493,885	$ 1,579,196
July	14,910,104	4,889,726	4,288,382
August	12,606,259	4,574,312	4,327,699
Totals	$41,590,788	$12,957,923	$10,195,277

*Includes clothing, household replacements, day and sleep away camp, and incidentals. Does not include regular bi-monthly grants.

Source: New York City Department of Welfare, *Monthly Statistical Reports,* June, July, and August 1963 and 1968.

B-WAC members paid a price for their activities, sometimes encountering physical abuse from authorities. Ultimately, they won concessions from New York City welfare administrators, and their actions fostered less restrictive policies and services provided in a respectful manner at public assistance offices.

Mainstream civil rights groups were reluctant to join or aid women from the lowest economic class. Like most of society, they too blamed grant-income women for being poor. Presumably, civil rights activists were angry that welfare recipients were speaking out about their plight—and even organizing, and demanding larger allocations or jobs.[4]

As B-WAC matured, its members joined school and hospital boards, parent–teachers associations, and political clubs. Middle-class bureaucrats were quickly made aware that—rather than administering for and to the poor—they would henceforth have to cooperate with the poor. Although there were instances of stalemates on important issues at community and other meetings, agenda items were addressed. The culture and language of the "ins" were reflective of their comfortable lives. Well-off people attempted to understand the language of poverty. In spite of a turbulent beginning, the stage was set for cooperation between ethnically diverse groups from different classes—a coalition that was a credit to the many people within it.

B-WAC existed only from 1967 to 1973, yet its principals helped to mobilize large numbers of people. They coordinated a considerable amount of human energy by means of sit-ins, marches, and confrontations with social service officials, the mayor, and congresspersons. Through B-WAC, welfare recipients had a voice that could join others in advocating a better life for the people who were on the bottom of the economic strata.

To determine the results of these efforts, it is necessary to examine the events leading to the creation of B-WAC. A historical overview and a description of the welfare system in the 1960s are provided in subsequent chapters.

Four main assumptions have guided this research:

1. The women receiving public assistance were motivated to organize for social, political, and economic benefits. They wished to increase opportunities for their children, and to join the mainstream of America.

2. Fresh insight regarding the needs and concerns of urban female recipients would emerge from the study.

3. It was also expected to expand social scientists' perspective relating to community activists who are women of color.

4. The literature on poor people's movements would be augmented.

Among the questions under study were:

— What was the motivation for establishing B-WAC?

— What were its strengths and weaknesses?

— Was its members' political orientation generally radical or conservative, and were they feminists?

— Did the recipients, organizers, and theorists have the same goals?

— Did the movement have an impact on local or national social policy?

— Will organization or mobilization best advance the concerns of low- and grant-income people?

— Was the movement's demise unique among grass roots protest groups?

— Can social planners design programs that encourage community leadership and personal development by adopting strategies used by the B-WAC participants?

METHODOLOGY

This book examines the weaknesses, strengths, and strategies of an important vehicle for social change in the 1960s. The research is based largely on personal interviews with B-WAC leaders and an analysis of the original minutes, correspondence, and newsletters of the organization. A total of 39 individuals were interviewed, in these three categories: (1) welfare rights recipients; (2) theorists, staff, and organizers; and (3) public officials and New York City Depart-

ment of Welfare staff. Paraphrased responses of the interviewees are provided throughout the study. The names of the
respondents have been changed, except where both the first
and last names are given at first appearance. A broad and
open-ended format was used with the interviewees to facilitate
maximum memory recovery. We discussed members' and
organizers' motivations and participation; the nonviolent disruptive tactics that they employed; the merits of mobilization
and organization; the movement's impact on social welfare
policy; and whether these same methods can be adopted by
social planners today. Additional data are axiomatic in that
"the story is the data."[5]

I seek to determine the strengths and deficiencies of B-WAC
in the context of mobilization and organization theory regarding poor people's social change activities, motivations, and
group interests.

Chapter 2 explores the nature and the historical development of the welfare bureaucracy. A description of New York
City's economic, political, and welfare systems in the 1960s
examines briefly the political motivations of the Lindsay administration and specific officials. I have attempted to provide
a clearer picture of the political arena and its impact on the
activists by discussing the various citywide political antagonists
and protagonists. The section on Brooklyn life characterizes,
interprets, and focuses on the connections between New York
City as a whole and life in one of its boroughs.

The philosophy and background of the movement's white
middle-class professional organizers are depicted and examined in Chapter 3. Also, their recruitment and mobilizing
efforts are chronicled and documented. Finally, the
relationship of the Catholic church to the community organizers is addressed, in addition to the black church's posture concerning welfare rights actions.

In Chapter 4 strategies utilized to attract other clients to the
movement are documented and analyzed. In addition, the
contributions of the Volunteers in Service to America (VISTA)

are discussed. This segment strives to illustrate the diversity of the institutions and people involved in the welfare rights efforts. Their role is reviewed, and the chapter focuses on the federal government's community development activities during the 1960s.

An examination of the dynamics surrounding the proliferation of neighborhood groups, and the genesis of the Brooklyn Welfare Action Council are provided in Chapter 5. Attention is focused on the B-WAC demonstrations and the mobilizing strategies associated with them; in addition, coalition building by the activists is addressed. The results of that effort together with the weaknesses and strengths of B-WAC are documented and examined.

A summary of the findings and recommendations constitute a portion of Chapter 6. Interviews with former recipient-leaders and excerpts from newsletters and articles are included.

NOTES

1. B-WAC—voted into existence by organized welfare clients in November 1967—was a member of the National Welfare Rights Organization (NWRO), a coalition of all welfare rights groups around the country. In addition, B-WAC was part of the Manhattan-based New York Citywide Coordinating Council of Welfare Rights Groups (Citywide), a coordinating body for groups in all the New York City boroughs (Manhattan, Bronx, Queens, Brooklyn, and Staten Island). In 1968 there was a short-lived New York State organization (New York State Welfare Rights Organization—NYS-WRO). The purpose of NWRO—founded in 1966—was to facilitate and coordinate efforts to reform and eventually replace the nation's welfare system with a guaranteed annual income for all Americans. The welfare rights hierarchy in Brooklyn, New York, was as follows: local neighborhood welfare rights organizations, B-WAC, Citywide, NYS-WRO, and NWRO.

2. The numbers contradict Richard Cloward and Frances Fox Piven's estimate in *Poor People's Movements: Why They Succeed, How They Fail* (New York: Vintage Books, 1979), p. 226. Since their data are presumably from NWRO records, they do not offer the complete picture. Brooklyn members frequently disagreed with NWRO policies or stands and refused to pay NWRO dues. Consequently, at any given time, a little over half the

Brooklyn participants were listed in the national office.

3. From New York City Department of Welfare, *Monthly Statistical Reports*, June, July, and August 1968.

4. A respondent interviewed in the summer of 1983 in Brooklyn, New York, noted that some civil rights leaders were uncomfortable with welfare rights organizing because it lessened the impact of civil rights efforts. Further, to the dismay of middle-class activists, many observers did not differentiate between the two movements, assuming that the two were connected. Welfare rights organizations (WROs) were similar to the unpopular anarchists of the 1930s. The 1960s respectable movements disavowed WRO actions and the organization itself. In sum, civil rights activists were embarrassed about vocal, out-of-the-closet recipients.

5. John Hartman and Jack Hedblom, *Methods for the Social Sciences: A Handbook for Students and Non-Specialists* (Westport, Conn.: Greenwood Press, 1979), p. iii.

2

The Nature of America's and New York City's Welfare Systems

SOCIAL WELFARE IN THE UNITED STATES

The social welfare issues that surfaced in the 1960s had their roots in the colonial era, especially in the English Poor Laws of 1601. No charitable trusts or welfare institutions existed in seventeenth-century America. Life was hard in the young cities and on the frontiers, leaving many colonists temporarily or permanently destitute — particularly those who had arrived nearly penniless. From the beginning, in the seventeenth century, the care of poor people had a threefold purpose: (1) providing succor to neighbors without means to obtain or maintain basic human necessities; (2) assisting individuals to regain or obtain employment; and (3) decreasing the threat of civil unrest. The first two responses by the predominantly middle and upper classes were encouraged by religious teachings and a sense of civic responsibility, and the last issue stemmed from political considerations.[1]

The existence of a Poor Law in England and its subsequent adoption in America secured the individual's right to public assistance and acknowledged the government's obligation in that area. Still, its role was somewhat ambiguous between the seventeenth and nineteenth centuries. Its practice varied from tax collections and distributions of funds to needy persons through churches and charitable agencies, to assuming total responsibility for the care of families in crises.[2] Poverty was regarded as a moral issue, and it was thought to result from moral flaws or other forms of physical and moral weakness. With work plentiful and labor scarce, the prevailing eighteenth-century view was that paupers were lazy or unwilling to work and improve their lot. Consequently—noted Walter Trattner—some people advocated letting them starve. Moreover,

> The condition of all welfare recipients, regardless of need or cause should be worse than that of the lowest paid self-supporting laborer. While relief should not be denied the poor life should be made so miserable for them that they would rather work than accept public aid.[3]

The Poor Law Reform Bill of 1834 in England institutionalized punitive attitudes toward the English poor, which were also accepted in America.

> Poor relief was redesigned to increase fear of insecurity, rather than to check its causes or even to alleviate its problems. At best it would prevent starvation or death from exposure, but it would do so as economically and unpleasantly as possible. The measure of the system's soundness would be its deterrent effect.[4]

Opponents of this law believed that the public relief system tended to demoralize recipients, depress their standard of living, and promote dependency. These concepts were accepted by welfare recipients themselves, well into the 1960s.

Native Americans—named Indians by the European settlers—typically received no assistance before 1860 because many white people considered them savages. Similarly, slaves were their masters' responsibility. When the Civil War ended,

African-Americans' problems were handled by the Bureau of Refugees, Freedmen, and Abandoned Lands, a program established in 1865 by Congress and administered by the War Department. This "Freedman's Bureau" was the nation's first federally funded welfare program. Poor white southerners received segregated service from the same agency, which lasted until 1871, after which the states assumed responsibility for public dependents who were institutionalized. But poor people living outside almshouses, hospitals, schools, and other institutions were completely dependent on private charity. Cultural societies were established for the purpose of caring for persons from specific ethnic backgrounds; any remaining funds were distributed to those of other nationalities. Only the Quakers routinely helped people of different faiths and backgrounds.

Free African-Americans of wealthy or modest means formed societies to assist former slaves. With the exception of the Quakers, no other religious/ethnic charitable organizations offered aid to people of African descent. Until the twentieth century, these poverty-stricken Americans relied on private individual assistance and a small number of segregated city or state institutions for help.

Aid in the Twentieth Century

Categorical assistance and forced institutionalization of unworthy applicants in workhouses emerged in the 1800s. Home relief—which continues to exist in 1988—was obtained by deserving paupers. Assistance provided in this manner assumed major importance in a system that had originally given aid to everyone in need.

This new system enabled welfare administrators to separate and designate specific groups of people for aid or employment programs. Hence, officials gained additional control over the lives of poor people. Their power has continued into the twentieth century. In the 1960s, women of color who were lacking life's basics found themselves in an untenable position. The acquisition of funds in the category to which they were assigned—although theoretically for the worthy—(Aid to Dependent Children) forced them to live a difficult life because society viewed these women as the unworthy poor. They were not widows, but victims of their mates' and the country's structural unemployment problems—as well as racial and gender prejudice.

Applying for Assistance in New York

By 1964, the assistance categories—all of which required a means test to determine financial status and eligibility—had expanded to seven and were administered by the New York State Department of Public Welfare through 30 citywide welfare centers. Home Relief and Veteran Assistance received only state and local funding. The remaining categories, which had federal allocations, included:

Aid to the Disabled

Old Age Assistance (65 years old or over)

Assistance to the Blind

Medical Assistance to the Blind

Medical Assistance for the Aged

Aid to Dependent Children (ADC)

By 1965, Aid to Dependent Children had become the largest of the programs. Indeed, from colonial times, the biggest expenditure of public relief funds has been for widows, orphans, and illegitimate children. During that early era, the latter item consumed an average of 35 percent of all municipal monies.[5]

In 1968, because welfare remained a state rather than a federal responsibility, ADC grants and the number of welfare cases were especially low in southern states. According to the *Bedford-Stuyvesant-New York Recorder* of January 3, 1969, "Welfare in Alabama is where you go when you're going nowhere." According to the article, a family of four on ADC received a $177 monthly check for food, shelter, and clothing. Federal funds accounted for 83 percent of the grant. In 1967 Alabama forfeited $11.6 million in federal monies because it refused to contribute matching funds amounting to 17 percent of the total cost. At the other end of the spectrum was New York City, where welfare grants were higher. According to New York City's *Monthly Public Assistance Summary 1960–1973*, yearly payments in 1969 for a family of four (including rent) were $3,408. The U.S. Department of Labor noted that a family of four in 1969 required $4,000 a year to live above the poverty line.[6] New York provided grants that were 15 percent — compared to Alabama's 53 percent — below the poverty line. Moreover, New York State law authorized additional funds for such special needs as furniture, clothing, washing machines, paint, camp, and air conditioners for asthmatics and all people with lung problems. Few New York City clients knew of such provisions, and rarely did they receive additional money for any reason. As will be illustrated, organizers of recipients used these regulations for recruiting purposes (see Table 1.1).

Recipients and Staff Victims of the System

Whether in New York or Alabama, having one's welfare application approved by administrators involved delay and aggravation. Applicants normally made several round trips to the welfare center with birth or death certificates, utilities, bills and school and medical records. Perseverance was a requisite to be approved for aid. However, acceptance onto the welfare rolls did not end the hardships. Although money for basic needs would henceforth be relatively secure, welfare recipients paid a costly psychological price because degrading and patronizing service was normal procedure at the welfare centers. Recipients noted that animals were treated better in the United States than poor people. Scenes in New York City offices varied little from those in other states before 1967, where rude behavior from state and local officials was accepted by the poor as part of the price of public assistance. Moreover, employees — as many a recipient correctly surmised — were not very financially dissimilar from the people that they served.

Staff at welfare offices in the late 1950s and early 1960s earned $5,000 a year, with benefits; but that was just 20 percent above the federal poverty line. Ms. Quall, a caseworker, explained in an interview that workers "finally received decent wages as a result of the 1968 strike by the Social Service Employees Union." Prior to this job action, welfare center staff earned little more than their clients. After the strike, benefits were expanded. Staff could attend college tuition-free, while continuing to receive wages and maintain eligibility for promotions. First-level supervisors could then receive $13,000 yearly. The four staff members whom I interviewed received masters' degrees while city employees, as did many of their colleagues.

New York City Welfare Centers

The physical space at the welfare centers exacerbated the problems. Walls were a dirty green or beige; desks and chairs were old and needed repair. The unspeakably repulsive toilets often flooded and there were almost never any tissues. Personnel facilities were only slightly better. With little or no privacy, staff sat hunched over their desks trying to confer with clients as quietly as possible. Further aggravation arose from the fact that the staff — predominantly young white men and women recently out of undergraduate school and with only a limited experience of black and Hispanic people — were uncomfortable with this reduction of their personal space. According to my interviewees, staff responded to the situation by asserting their authority in ways so disrespectful to recipients that it generated an atmosphere of mutual dislike and distrust. Former staff employees observed that the system's size and paperwork requirements discouraged a nurturing, sympathetic approach to service. Therefore, in a system that was demeaning to them both, the two natural allies were on opposing sides of the welfare issue.

An Impersonal System

Shared economic problems notwithstanding, welfare staff members were in America's mainstream. Their attitudes mirrored the nation's prejudices concerning persons believed to be lacking in a fully developed work ethic. Consequently, in seventeenth-century tradition, welfare services were provided in a manner geared toward making a client's life as uncomfortable as possible, in order to force the recipient to obtain employment.

This strategy might have been useful if there had been other alternatives for recipients. But most New York City clients were essentially unemployable in the 1960s, due to never having worked outside the home, and to having to care for children or disabled adults. The small number of employable people on welfare were unskilled, and few had high school diplomas. In 1965, for example, employable persons constituted only 3.8 percent of the people on welfare. Of that number, 14.9 percent had never worked outside the home.[7]

Despite such statistics, the welfare bureaucracy was encouraged to keep the public assistance rolls low. Thus, in New York City in June, July, and August 1963, 45 percent of the cases were rejected;[8] but many more applicants were temporarily denied aid until they depleted their own resources. In the same period five years later — 1968 — a different picture emerged. An analysis reveals a 21 percent decrease in the number of people rejected, despite a 55 percent increase in applications (see Table 2.1).[9] Correspondingly, total grants in 1963 rose from $31,063,556 to a 1968 level of $152,728,014 — nearly a 500 percent increase.[10] This increase in acceptance and assistance levels was due in part to activities that will be described in Chapters 3, 4, and 5.

The denial of aid — even temporarily — posed hardships for

Table 2.1
Aid to Dependent Children, Citywide:
Number of New Cases and Total Grants

| | New Cases | |
	Applied	Accepted
1963		
June	4,312	52%
July	5,073	50
August	4,902	65
1968		
June	6,789	77%
July	9,500	78
August	9,286	81

| | Total Grants | |
	1963	1968
June	$10,240,384	$45,867,903
July	10,362,124	46,324,000
August	10,461,048	60,436,111

Source: New York City Department of Welfare, *Monthly Statistical Reports*, 1963, 1968.

people, then as now. Loans from friends and relatives either receiving assistance or in the working poor category were their only recourse, interviewees explained. When grants did begin to arrive, a large portion had to be used for loan repayments, while utilities and other accounts were left unpaid, As a result, clients often experienced increased—rather than less—financial difficulties.

Theory, Reality, and Practice

The response of the United States to people in financial crises has been to create a system of constituent dependency. The unspoken mandate has been to maintain social and political order and the work ethic. As Cloward and Piven noted:

Relief policies are cyclical, liberal or restrictive depending on the problems of regulation in the larger society with which government must contend.[11]

According to an April 1964 three-page report called *Information Regarding the New York City Department of Public Welfare*, the department's[12] three main objectives were:

1. To meet the common human needs (either in whole or in part) of those individuals who are unable to help themselves;
2. To return persons to gainful employment or assist them toward self-support and a maximum of self-care; and
3. To prevent dependency.

When I interviewed women who had survived 10–15 years on welfare grants, they maintained that the system did not follow its mandate. For instance, complaints were numerous about forced temporary low-wage employment with little opportunity for advancement and no job security. Such employment intensified the pressures already on families by reducing the amount of parental supervision. And unlike the typical reward system for most Americans, welfare mothers could not augment their grants by accepting additional, outside work. Instead, welfare allocations were lowered to reflect the recipients' changed financial status. When a job ended, readjustments by the department were slow, and recipients endured hardships while waiting for the correction to be made.

Fair hearings were the primary area of redress for clients — that is, for those who were aware of the procedure — but this had its own problems. Statements were required from lawyers, clergy, and social workers in support of a recipient's claim that being underbudgeted was a severe hardship. Clients risked permanently losing part of their grants if these testimonies were not provided. When budget complaints subsided for a week or a month, Welfare Department policy required staff to assume that the client had obtained funds from other sources. On the basis of that assumption, all revision activities would be dropped by the department. Instead, it would begin investigating the possible existence of unreported income.

Problems such as these were communicated among recipients. In effect, they stood as a warning about volunteering for any program recommended by the department. Consequently, of the women I interviewed, 90 percent acknowledged having known people on welfare who resisted accepting employment unless they were certain to be leaving the welfare rolls completely.

Working — with the department's knowledge — at subsistence-level wages guaranteed the client a double life: half in the mainstream, and half on public assistance through supplementary grants. All services were reduced in that case, and yet the recipient's activities would continue to be monitored. "Such conditions, including low wage jobs, delayed grant adjustments added support to Piven's and Cloward's statements about the system's insensitivity and its regulatory mandate," noted a respondent.

NEW YORK CITY ECONOMIC, POLITICAL, AND WELFARE ENVIRONMENT IN THE 1960s

President John F. Kennedy signed the Public Welfare amendments to the Social Security Act on July 25, 1962. These amendments essentially provided for increased federal funds to states and enabled them to expand job training, placement, and casework to recipients. The law's proponents saw it as an effort to personalize the system and put able-bodied people to work. Opponents viewed the law as a method of changing the person to fit the system, while leaving the system's deficiencies intact.

In 1965, the Economic Opportunity Act (EOA) was passed, and the Office of Economic Opportunity (OEO) was established. As reported in the media, the act was a major weapon in the war against poverty, and it required that seven programs be created and operated by OEO: Volunteers in Service to America, or VISTA (a domestic Peace Corps); Job Corps, for high school dropouts; Upward Bound, which assisted bright students living in the ghettos to obtain college entrance; Neighborhood Youth Corps, for unemployed youngsters; Operation Head Start, which offered preschool training; a program of grants and loans to low-income rural families and migrant workers; and the Community Action Program (CAP), which encouraged maximum feasible participation of community residents in the campaign to revitalize neighborhood institutions and identify local resources.

This "war against poverty"—as the EOA was popularly called—reached New York City neighborhoods amid considerable fanfare, providing a limited number of first-time white-collar–type jobs for some residents. Hope for the future spread through the poorer areas when low-income people saw next-door neighbors staffing community programs. Until that time, most administrators had lived outside the area, regardless of ethnic background.

Recipients on the economic bottom availed themselves of the new services, but did not share the community's general euphoria. Their lives remained virtually unchanged. With no skills or training and a modicum of formal education, welfare clients realized that they were moving further away from the mainstream of American life. They watched other classes making progress. "In our isolation, we blamed ourselves and complained about welfare-related problems," says Ms. Delta, a welfare rights and community activist.

Society as a whole remained disdainful of people on public assistance. Sympathy for recipients would have meant acknowledging that the U.S. cultural and economic system had serious flaws. Amid this hopelessness, a new politician surfaced. He was to give fresh meaning to the war on poverty.

In 1965, John V. Lindsay campaigned for New York City mayor on a progressive platform that, among other issues, addressed the concerns of low- and grant-income people in addition to those of the middle class. His election brought renewed enthusiasm to the poor of the nation's largest city, as we shall see.

CITYWIDE POLITICAL ANTAGONISTS AND PROTAGONISTS

Some influential people in and outside the public assistance bureaucracy were exceptions to the general malaise. In principle, their views concerning the system's weaknesses paralleled those held by welfare rights advocates. Nicholas Kisburg, legislative director of the International Brotherhood of Teamsters, wrote in an April 26, 1968, letter to New York Governor Nelson Rockefeller:

> The New York City welfare system is bankrupt of ideas and money and it is now incumbent on you to initiate such legislation as will enable you to put the local Social Services Department into receivership, just as the courts would in the instance of an insolvent business.[13]

Welfare administrators knew about the system's shortcomings, including that the amount of grants fell 12 percent short of providing subsistence to families. One administrator observed:

> We tell people we are going to help them. Yet we don't pay them enough to meet their needs, we penalize them for trying to keep their families together. We say we do — but can't really — offer social services which would help them live economically, help them find jobs, education and job training. The entire system is designed to perpetuate the dependency, and keep them in their place.[14]

John Lindsay — despite his popularity among poor people and minorities — was beset by insurrections in the ghettos in 1966, and in welfare centers in 1967. Furthermore, he was having to contend with throngs of young white affluent dropouts who were defying authority in every way possible. They demonstrated for such causes as an end to the Vietnam War, and civil rights for people of color. These young whites held love-ins in the city's parks and participated in the squatters' movement, among other actions. New York City streets and neighborhoods teemed with people, and with twice that many ideas and plans. Often, OEO funds were used to translate some of these notions into community programs.

Mayor Lindsay sensed the inherent potential for both violence and peaceful change in the city. Striving for peace, he would periodically walk through the ghettos to get the feel of the city's pulse. Residents were impressed by his visits — although mainly Lindsay just listened to complaints, and promised nothing. Still, he had come to their neighborhoods and heard the problems firsthand, allowing residents to vent their emotions. Little else was to be expected, according to people who lived in the area. Middle class residents, however, were the ones who managed to secure city jobs through the staffing of poverty and community action programs.

The people hired during Lindsay's tenure bore little

resemblance to the average city employee or politician. Many were people from the communities or young 1960s activists. These new recruits brought fresh energy to the efforts aimed at improving life for New York's marginal and disenfranchised residents.

Of all the Lindsay appointees, Mitchell Svirdoff probably had the most direct impact on poor people. A man with a working-class background and a former Connecticut labor leader, Svirdoff established New York City's Human Resources Administration (HRA) in 1966 and was its first commissioner.[15] This was also the year that New York State's total welfare expenditures passed the $1 billion mark.[16] HRA was one of the first superagencies of its type in the United States, and became a model for other cities. Svirdoff created a giant bureaucracy that encompassed the majority of New York City social service — including the Department of Public Welfare — and community programs under the auspices of one agency. But Svirdoff, who was a power broker, had many functions. His symbolic hats were diverse. His "entire city hat" — as HRA head — was sometimes replaced by a "borough hat." Svirdoff's involvement in Brooklyn affairs was enormous, as will be shown. First, however, a brief review of some major Brooklyn neighborhood agencies in low-income areas.

BROOKLYN'S COMPETING COMMUNITY AGENCIES

In 1967 the primary community development corporation in Brooklyn's Bedford Stuyvesant area[17] was Youth in Action (YIA), through which a substantial portion of federal funds was channeled. Almost all the neighborhood's social and community development programs received grants from YIA, except welfare rights. The latter and a few grass roots organizations concluded that YIA's community responsibilities took second place to furthering the careers of certain well-connected individuals. Welfare rights advocates had little contact with the agency, and even less knowledge of its activities.

Svirdoff and other City Hall power brokers reached a similar conclusion about YIA. As a result, the Bedford-Stuyvesant Restoration Corporation (Restoration) was formed and became the conduit for community development funds, which were obtained largely through the EOA and the efforts of Senator Robert Kennedy—thus bypassing YIA. Nevertheless, as one respondent described the situation,

> Welfare Rights and other community people were disturbed that outsiders, led by Svirdoff in cooperation with a few upper class residents, could circumvent YIA, a community organization. They recognized the situation as a middle class venture. Nonetheless, since most activists believed the project would enhance the Bedford-Stuyvesant community, they reluctantly decided against participating in YIA's struggle for the funds. In hindsight, some welfare rights advocates felt they were mistaken to abandon YIA, because they soon discovered that Brooklyn Restoration's structure reflected the same middle class concepts of public assistance recipients as the rest of the city.

All of the former organizers and 13 of the leaders agreed with that statement, but 2 of them were pleased with the WROs' position and had no second thoughts about the maneuver. Many advocates of community control blamed Svirdoff for the ensuing problems, contending that he had acted in an unsuitable manner. Svirdoff was disliked and praised by an equal number of residents.

While some grass roots needs were addressed by Restoration—referral services and counseling—by and large its programs focused on issues concerning working poor and middle-income people. The traditional, paternalistic services approach—so demeaning to grant- and low-income people—was again established. Grass roots organizations blamed themselves for allowing this phenomenon to occur in their community. Restoration's organizational structure was developed by socially and financially secure people, who in turn installed Franklin Thomas – a former police officer and lawyer – as its president.[18] Apparently, Restoration's influential constituents wanted a substantive role in local, state, and national affairs. Thomas's responsibility was to facilitate that effort. Community people without educational credentials and no access to powerful people received limited service. Welfare rights' self-imposed isolation – ostensibly for Brooklyn's own good[19] – left these activists powerless to affect Restoration's policy. Thus, three distinct community institutions existed in the area: the welfare rights organizations (see Chapter 1, note 1), Bedford-Stuyvesant Restoration, and YIA. And each ignored the others.

YIA – its reputation further tarnished by having lost the battle to Restoration – was occupied with developing strategies that would be useful in regaining constituents and power. Service to grant-income people was left to the WROs. The organizations in question never met to discuss their common interests. Each worked for its own clients: the aspiring middle class, the working poor people, and the welfare recipients. Respondents suggested that, had the groups collaborated on community and citywide issues, Brooklyn could have forged a powerful coalition with long-range effects on its residents and people around the country.

THE CULTURAL AND ECONOMIC DYNAMICS OF BROOKLYN LIFE

In 1970, Brooklyn (County of Kings) was the largest borough in New York City, with a population of 2,627,319 or 33.8 percent of all New York City residents (see Table 2.2). Had it been a separate city, it would have been the third largest in America. Black and Hispanic residents were 25 percent and 14.5 percent of Brooklyn's population, respectively.[20]

Within its 81 square miles, Brooklyn is a borough of contrasts, including numerous residential neighborhoods with

Table 2.2
Population of New York State,
New York City (All Boroughs),
Brooklyn, and Manhattan, 1960 and 1970

	New York State	New York City (All Boroughs)	Brooklyn	Manhattan
1960	16,782,304	7,781,984	2,627,319	1,698,281
1970	18,241,391	7,895,563	2,601,974	1,539,233

Source : New York City Department of City Planning, data compiled from the U.S. Department of Commerce, Bureau of the Census, 1960 and 1970.

stately homes and mansions sprinkled along tree-lined thoroughfares. There are middle and lower economic-class row houses, and communities with nationally renowned brownstone homes. Some areas have medium- and high-rise rental buildings with apartments the size of small homes. Brooklyn has its own museums, parks, a botanical garden, zoo, the Academy of Music, public and private colleges, and trade schools. Moreover, the Brooklyn Catholic diocese is the second largest in the nation. New Yorkers have called it the borough of churches since early in the nineteenth century.

On the other hand, some neighborhoods have substandard housing, high crime, and abandoned squalor. Residents in such areas — often people of color — live without adequate services. The institutions — health, education, and social services — are weaker than in middle-class areas of the borough. A substantial number of the low-income residents there — nearly 40 percent — receive public assistance.[21] According to the New York City Department of City Planning, the 1970 median income of areas with substantial black and Hispanic population was $5,825 — at least $3,000 less than the boroughwide average.[22] A case can be made that a major portion of that percentage must be credited to these neglected neighborhoods. Female-headed families numbered 45,550, with 69,823 male-headed households.[23] Again, it can be maintained that the female-headed families reside primarily in low-income areas.

Statistics reveal the grim conditions under which these women and children lived. According to the 1970 census tract, *Income Characteristics of the Population*, the mean income for families on public assistance in Brooklyn was $2,192, with $10,181 being the mean income for the borough (see Table 2.3).[24] The national statistics for 1970 — as listed on Table 2.4 — were comparable, with yearly public assistance payments of $2,256; 23 percent of the population had incomes of $15,000 and over.

Of the Brooklyn families receiving public assistance, 36 percent had related children under the age of 18 living with them; 37 percent of these had related children under the age of 6.[25] Females

Table 2.3
NYC Income Characteristics, 1969

	BROOKLYN	MANHATTAN
	MEAN INCOME	
All Families	$10,181	$9,635
Public Assistance Recipients	2,192	2,244
	PERCENT OF FAMILIES BELOW POVERTY LINE*	
All Families	13.9%	15.5%
	PERCENT OF FAMILIES RECEIVING PUBLIC ASSISTANCE	
	38.9%	45.3%

*United States Department of Labor: Poverty Line $4,000 for urban renters, family of four at lower level of living.

Source: U.S. Department of Commerce, Bureau of the Census, *Income Characteristics of the Population: 1970* (Washington, D.C.: Government Printing Office, 1970).

Table 2.4
National Income Statistics

	PA**	Aid to Dependent Children (Families)
1970	$14,434,000	$4,853,000
1960	4,042,000	1,056,000

Average Monthly Payments to
Aid to Dependent Children Families

1970	=	$187.95
1960	=	108.35

Percent Gross National Product
for Social Welfare Expenditures***

1970	=	15%
1960	=	11

Percent Family Income

Under 3,000 a year

	1970	1960
Black	20	47
White	7	19

Under 15,000 a year

	1970	1960
Black	10	1
White	24	4

**PA includes: Aid to Dependent Children, Old Age Assistance, Aid to the Disabled, General Assistance, Aid to the Blind.

***Social Welfare Expenditures include: Railroad Retirement & Unemployment Insurance, State Unemployment Insurance and Services, Health and Medical, Housing, Institutional Care, Workmen's Compensation, Public Employee Retirement, Public Assistance and Education.

Source : U.S. Department of Commerce, Bureau of the Census, *Historical Statistics of the United States, Colonial Times to 1970*, Vol. 2 (Washington, D.C.: Government Printing Office, 1975).

headed the households in 45 percent of the cases, with 40 percent parenting children under 18 years old.[26] Most Brooklyn residents were between the ages of 20 and 34 (see Table 2.5).

Female single-parent households encountered numerous barriers. Many of these women — overweight,[27] uneducated, and unskilled — sometimes obtained outside employment as domestics or child-care providers. But much of their days were spent waiting in line for various services. In particular, welfare and medical office staff would instruct clients to arrive hours before the professional ever appeared. Respondents recalled that employees at institutions serving poverty areas did not consider a poor person's time important. This phenomenon extended to every aspect of the clients' lives: When summoned by school officials regarding a wayward son or daughter, they would have to wait; the same situation existed for them at all service agencies. These long-standing issues supported the perception that institutions created to serve the poor were often barriers to improving their condition. Support for this assertion is implicit in the organizers' and theorists' comments that will be reported in Chapter 3. In addition, an examination of the Catholic church's role is offered there, illustrating the fundamental conflict between the church and its activist clergy.

Table 2.5
Population Characteristics in Selected Brooklyn Neighborhoods, 1970

Communities With Major Welfare Rights Organizing	Total Population	Percent Black Population	Total Families	Persons Per Family	Percent Total Married (Not Separated)	Median Age	Median Income	Percent Spanish Language Population
Bedford-Stuyvesant	196,963	81%	44,448	3	45	23	$5,257	17%
Brownsville	122,378	73	27,654	4	46	19	5,024	23
Bushwick	137,870	30	33,428	4	52	23	5,642	35
Crown Heights	101,080	55	25,974	3	52	31	7,084	11
Flatbush	149,801	22	41,576	3	58	34	8,193	8
Fort Green	111,671	42	24,671	2	55	28	5,874	21
Red Hook	277,856	14	67,878	3	55	28	6,460	27
Williamsburg	179,454	9	45,007	3	55	26	5,888	37

Source: New York City Department of City Planning, data compiled from the U.S. Department of Commerce, Bureau of the Census, 1970.

NOTES

1. From Walter Trattner, *From Poor Law to Welfare State: A History of Social Welfare in America* (New York: Free Press, 1974).

2. By 1971 a person's right to assistance had been successfully challenged and eliminated; it had become a privilege granted by local governments to the selected worthy poor. The categories of the worthy poor included widows, orphans, the sick, and the elderly; unworthy poor were sturdy beggars and the unemployed. Funds were provided either indoors — at institutions that cared for the indigent (for example, hospitals and almshouses) — on outdoors — that is, by direct payments to the individual or family in need. The system is essentially the same in 1988.

3. Trattner, *From Poor Law to Welfare State*, p. 52.

4. Ibid., p. 47.

5. Ibid., p. 28.

6. U.S. Department of Labor Employment and Training Division, Bureau of Labor Statistics, *Regional Manpower Administration Notice #1-72*, press release, March 17, 1969. However, in 1967, the Labor Department had noted that renters in the lowest levels of living needed $5,915 for an urban family of four to stave off poverty.

7. *Welfarer* (January—February 1966): 15.

8. New York City Department of Welfare, *Monthly Statistical Reports*, June, July, and August 1963.

9. Ibid., June, July, and August 1968.

10. Ibid., June, July, and August 1963 and 1968.

11. Richard Cloward and Frances Fox Piven, *Regulating the Poor: The Functions of Social Welfare* (New York: Vintage Books, 1971), p. xiii.

12. In 1988, the name of the New York City public assistance office is the Human Resources Administration, Department of Social Services. I shall refer to the Welfare Department throughout this book.

13. Quoted in the Brooklyn Catholic weekly, the *Tablet*, May 2, 1968, p. 13.

14. Ibid. This view was supported by 98 percent of the respondents in my study. The remaining 2 percent asserted that the department functioned as effectively as possible, given the statutory and political constraints.

15. From the author's 1984 interview with Mitchell Svirdoff.

16. New York State Department of Social Service, Bureau of Data Management and Analysis, "Milestones in Public Welfare in New York State 1626–1978," program brief #2, September 1979.

17. Brooklyn's Bedford Stuyvesant neighborhood is similar to the borough as a whole, with its contrasting poor and middle-class sections. Its residents are chiefly U.S. and Caribbean blacks. See the section "The Cultural and Economic Dynamics of Brooklyn Life" — later in the chapter — for details.

18. Franklin Thomas, who headed Restoration, is currently (1988) the president of the Ford Foundation. Efforts were made to interview him, but he was unavailable.

19. Like most of its residents, Brooklyn activists were fiercely loyal to the borough. Thus, they stayed out of the funding controversy so as to permit the funds to come into the area. Threats regarding the withdrawal of the Kennedy gift were ever present, so protracted opposition would have jeopardized the funding along with plans for the neighborhood's restoration. The extent to which Brooklyn residents actually benefited from the gift and whether there was any long-term impact for more than just a few upper-middle-class people are issues that are debatable and worthy of extensive research.

20. U.S. Department of Commerce, Bureau of the Census, *Income Characteristics of the Population: 1970* (Washington, D.C.: Government Printing Office, 1970); data compiled and treated by the New York Department of City Planning.

21. U.S. Dept. of Commerce, *Income Characteristics: 1970*.

22. Ibid.

23. Ibid.

24. Ibid.

25. Ibid.

26. Ibid.

27. "Welfare fat" is the term used to describe these women. Their weight problem stems from a diet that consists mainly of starch, because it's filling and staves off hunger.

3

Activists and Resources of a Movement

To organize welfare clients as well as the working poor was the idea of two social scientists, Frances Fox Piven and Richard Cloward. They developed theories suggesting that organizers and low-income people, together with community activists, could work to reduce social inequities. The problems encountered by welfare recipients and staff—due in part to the bureaucracy's size—were a perfect environment in which to test their ideas. In concert with CORE activist George Wiley,[1] Cloward and Piven fostered a national movement that had its roots in their article entitled "A Strategy to End Poverty" published in the *Nation* on May 2, 1966. In the article they discussed "the crisis theory of welfare reform." Specifically, they advanced the idea of organizing people who were eligible for welfare, as well as recipients, by demanding that welfare officials provide the maximum grants for clothing and other basic conveniences. Overloading the system was their strategy: Cloward and Piven reasoned that the welfare system would then collapse and be replaced with a national income plan. These grant requests were within the laws of social service departments around the country, and their hypothesis assumed that officials would meet the clients' needs as expressed. Therefore, applicants and recipients should organize and claim those allowances to which they were entitled. Such a campaign would be useful in getting large numbers of eligible people on the welfare rolls. As Cloward and Piven noted,

> It was a strategy designed to obtain immediate economic aid for the poor, coupled with the possibility of obtaining a longer term national income standard.[2]

Their basic concept was embraced by most organizers and welfare rights participants, with the latter group conquering their fears and confronting welfare officials in many major cities.

However, Cloward and Piven's disruptive tactics were not unilaterally accepted by all welfare rights organizers. For example, the Catholic clergy in Brooklyn suggested that the strategy exploited the poor. These church men and women believed that building an organization of dues-paying members would be more in the interest of poor people.[3] Cloward and Piven argued that mobilization and disruption were the main power sources of low-income people.[4] They pointed out that institutions were unaccustomed to operating in the midst of upheaval; with their routines shattered, business would be at a standstill.[5] Then poor and low-income people would be able to obtain official attention concerning their complaints.

Dispute over these two theories caused an ideological split between the scholars and the activists. However, both approaches were implemented around the country; and, as a result, they were instrumental in dislodging grants from the bureaucracy to welfare clients. Public assistance reached a peak in 1969. Witness the fact that, in 1963, special grants totaled $50,000 a month. But five years later — according to the New York *Times* on July 15, 1968 — welfare recipients in New York City were receiving $10–12 million a month. This was compelling evidence of the WROs' effectiveness. Social policy analysts correctly noted that the beneficiaries of those increased funds were basically people who had already been receiving welfare. One could argue that welfare rights' evidence of power, accompanied by publicity, was an integral factor in the turn of events. The strategy behind welfare rights organizing was to concentrate on nonrecipients and the working poor. There were two reasons for supporting this maneuver. First, theoretically, new applicants could more quickly overload the welfare system and destroy it. Second, an alliance could be forged between the working poor and recipients—thus enhancing the empowerment campaign. Since recipients were at the bottom and totally powerless and since poor people in general had minimal political or social influence, welfare rights theorists contended that coalitions among diverse ethnic and economic classes were vital to the drive for equity. On the other hand, perhaps the strategists had little confidence that recipients could be organized into a force warranting attention.

As the welfare rights movement matured, however, the tactics focused almost entirely on securing benefits—such as clothing and furniture grants—for current recipients. Major and sustained efforts for the purpose of recruiting new applicants did not occur,[6] and organizers continued to build welfare rights organizations with dues-paying members.

Hence, welfare rights became a most unique organization, and publicity brought it a measure of power. For example, an analysis of New York City's Aid to Dependent Children program discloses that in January 1966, out of 4,703 applications, 60.53 percent were accepted. Three years later—in January 1969—there were 7,212 applications and a 73.43 percent acceptance rate—a 13 percent increase.[7] While the numbers are less than overwhelming, they are significant. Further, Brooklyn's activity resulted in more people applying for assistance and being accepted in greater numbers throughout the five boroughs. People were more aware than before of the department's services, particularly the availability of one-time grants, which increased from $501,929 in July 1963 citywide to a high of $14,910,104 in July 1968 – a 2,800 percent increase (see Table 1.1). Like the citywide figure, Brooklyn's grants rose from $166,335 to $4,889,726 in 1963 and 1968, respectively.[8] There is little doubt that Brooklyn's activities had citywide impact. Recipients and other people in need took advantage of the department's permissiveness, fostered by organized clients – requesting and receiving funds that had been previously unavailable or unknown to them. In addition, temporarily unemployed workers obtained these funds for clothing, furniture, or rent without becoming full recipients of aid. In fact, during this era (1967–72), many poor people came to accept the idea that welfare was a right – not a privilege. Generally speaking, Brooklyn's contribution to improving the quality of life for low- and grant-income people brought the welfare system's weaknesses to the public stage for discussion and examination. As a result, throughout the city, people who were eligible for aid became more knowledgeable about the system and less ashamed of applying. Hence, the efforts of B-WAC members affected all recipients and working-class people.

The impact of their strategy was reflected in the attention that WROs' actions received from people outside the movement, especially persons and groups not on welfare. Unions, for example, included people who were affected by welfare rights activities, despite the fact that they distanced themselves from the WRO movement. One exception was the Social Service Employees Union (SSEU), which gave funds to welfare rights organizations and cooperated by joining picket lines and demonstrations.

THE BUREAUCRACY GAINS NEW STRENGTH

At the same time, the welfare bureaucracy itself was working to eliminate its structural weaknesses. When conservative politics returned, the welfare system was prepared. It easily reasserted itself; and a rejuvenated, streamlined administrative process emerged. Specifically, replacing minimum standards with one-time grants effectively stopped welfare rights organizing, because the WROs' major recruitment tool was eliminated. A blow had been dealt to the movement, but not before millions of dollars were put directly into the hands of grant-income people. Conversely, organizers, members, and theorists had underestimated the bureaucracy's strength and resiliency. Thus, its maneuvers to regain control by eliminating regulations and laws that threatened its existence surprised the clients, organizers, and theorists. Lacking any contingency plans, the response of welfare rights advocates was inadequate. They realized too late that the system's recovery forecasted the movement's demise. And that was a critical mistake.

In a 1983 interview, Richard Cloward acknowledged that the Brooklyn activists had been an example of a group that used its organizing skills and street protests to acquire substantial benefits for its members. But in discussing the movement's weaknesses, he explained that

WROs were consumed by its own organization, trying to institutionalize itself. Too much energy was put into building a membership organization. With poor people in the streets protesting, it was the moment to push for more benefits, not sign up members. The history of movements is that they start off militant with just a five to seven year life span, then a limited amount of recognition sets in and media leaders emerge. There's competition for publicity—squabbles are born—institutionalization sets in and militancy falls by the wayside. Media leaders forget how they gained recognition—when they abandon the tactic of protest, they also abandon the people who protested. The Civil Rights movement was different. Those activists got the voting rights bill. Then they moved from the streets to electoral politics. [Still] they should have continued in the streets as well as promoting electoral politics. The black poor had electoral leadership but no protest leadership.[9]

Cloward's last comment implies that elected officials tended to become settled and part of the establishment when their constituents neglected to hold them accountable. On the other hand, it is possible that he was referring to the fact that street protests enhance politicians' limited power, and thereby enable them to secure more benefits for their constituents. Cloward continued thus:

> If I were to do it again, I would oppose organizing people already on the rolls. I would push for organizing people not on the rolls. It would be an organization of poor people not just welfare clients. . . . A movement is not something one can do alone — one must have a coalition of various ethnic groups, classes and both sexes, including the unemployed, working poor, blue collar and middle class women and men, people of color and whites.[10]

In terms of street protests, Cloward's points have some merit. Authorities will respond when the bureaucracy is disrupted; how they react can vary from enforcement and arrests to avoidance and lack of acknowledgment. However, the risk of burnout is a paramount concern when protest strategies are central to the movement's activities. A person constantly puts her or his body on the line. Cloward did not explain how, what, or who would maintain the protesters' interests and high energy levels. With no organizational allegiance, protesters would have to maintain an intense loyalty to one or two persons. In that situation, movement theorists must develop plans to meet the imminent challenge of a demagogue who could sustain the required interest and support of street protests or mobilization. Moreover, since the issue itself would have to be sufficiently vital and intense to mobilize people, the privileged classes would likely view the group as a threat to their security, and would retaliate on a massive scale. Would the number of protesters be adequate to meet the power apparatus? With respect to numbers, perhaps an a priori question should be: How many people constitute a demonstration? Small protesting groups tend to invite violence because they are intimidating yet vulnerable. Cloward's response to the issue of violence is this:

> The protection for future movements is to get people of color to vote and be elected, [since the power structure] can't smash protestors if they vote.[11]

In other words, large numbers of politicians elected by and of low- and grant-income people can provide the demonstrators protection against harm by the establishment.

When asked about the strengths of welfare rights organizing, Cloward observed that the movement had elevated welfare to the status of a right, by creating an awareness among all people that everyone deserved the minimum conditions for a decent life "as a right not charity." Moreover, people now received funds that, in earlier years, they probably would not have gotten. The movement had educated people in activism, because welfare rights organizing was actually a training ground. It enabled people to use their skills for grass roots causes and interests. In fact, former WRO organizers are still active in their communities in 1988.

In sum, in the 1983 interview, Cloward opposed institutionalizing a movement, but advocated the use of traditional institutions — specifically the electoral system — to secure power and protection. Had welfare rights groups achieved institutionalization in the 1970s, they could have played a key role in the voter education and registration program of the 1980s. A vehicle to reach thousands of disenfranchised people would have been prepared and equipped to forge ahead for change. Many people would contend that relying on leaders in the establishment — elected or not — simply preserves a dependency that the protestors had sought to destroy. Power and dependency are contradictory, but related — since they both need one another. Overcoming the dilemma of that relationship will be difficult, short of insurgency.

BROOKLYN ORGANIZERS, NUNS, AND PRIESTS: MOBILIZING CLIENTS TO JOIN A NATIONAL ORGANIZATION

In 1966, Brooklyn's representatives to the first National Welfare Rights Conference in the District of Columbia returned home determined to establish local organizations throughout the borough. With assistance and encouragement from the liberal Catholic clergy, their efforts bore fruit. Within one year, storefront centers that addressed the problems of people receiving public aid were in almost every Brooklyn community where low-income people resided. This was a large and impressive accomplishment. However, as noted, the activist recipients did not work alone. Nuns and priests lent emotional and financial support so that clients could organize and administer an institution of their own.

First Welfare Rights Organizers

During the course of conducting a 1966 survey of community needs and problems, a group of Roman Catholic teaching nuns[12] met and became friends with women on welfare. It was en eye-opening experience for the nuns, who were mainly of Irish ancestry although New York born and bred. Normally suspicious of strangers, the poor opened their doors in welcome to these women representing the powerful Catholic church. Clients described to them the horrors of a welfare existence: stolen checks[13] that were not replaced for weeks; delayed approvals for relocation that resulted in apartments being lost or tenants evicted; and routine refusals of special allowances for shoes or winter coats.

When their survey was completed,[14] the nuns were not surprised to find that insufficient funds, inadequate housing, lack of child-care centers, and recurring fires, along with inadequate sanitation and police services, topped the list. The findings were supported by the problems that pupils brought to their parochial school every day. The nuns tried to help the students and their families on an individual basis. But it became clear that the "case-by-case approach to these issues provided only short-term solutions." The nuns reached a conclusion. "People on welfare had to organize for collective action," noted Sister Tina.[15]

Such thinking was radical, even in the liberalized environment of the Roman Catholic church at that time. But the nuns were determined to develop the principles set forth by the Second Vatican Council (1962–65) under Pope John XXIII. They couched their efforts in those concepts. They were mindful of the council's mandate that the church's activism should focus on the needs of the poor. The social dynamics of the 1960s — that is, the struggle for human and civil rights — also influenced the nuns, who interpreted these actions as an empowerment effort and a desire on the part of poor people in general and people of color specifically to help themselves.

A few weeks after the nun's survey was completed, a new priest arrived at Our Lady of Victory parish in Brooklyn's Bedford Stuyvesant section. Two years out of the seminary, the priest had acquired a reputation as a man of action, concerned about the plight of low-income people. Having served on the board of an antipoverty program in Queens — another borough of New York City — he left it because of disillusionment over corruption and infighting. His strong distrust of officials and politicians were to be adopted by the people that he would subsequently organize in Brooklyn.

Father Stevens joined Sisters Tina, Joan, and Ruth in organizing the welfare clients of Bedford Stuyvesant. They compiled additional information from neighboring parishes[16] where other priests were assisting tenants to implement rent strikes, and had achieved some successes. The nuns and Father Stevens believed that similar tactics would be effective against the Department of Public Welfare.

Organizing House by House

In the first week of February 1966, the three nuns assumed responsibility for a decrepit storefront[17] formerly used by members of a nearby convent. From that base they again surveyed[18] the neighborhood block by block to determine the financial status of residents, and they encouraged those on welfare to attend a meeting. Child-care services were offered as an inducement. A week later—with Father Stevens as chair—20 women on welfare attended the first of many meetings at the storefront office, which had undergone some cleaning and decorating by the nuns. Although there was widespread skepticism initially, those who attended went home more knowledgeable about their entitlements and about how the welfare bureaucracy functioned.

They learned, for example, that the New York State Social Services Department was legally bound to provide certain basic items, and that—once one had been accepted for welfare—it was within one's rights to request special allotments in order to purchase these commodities. This procedure was known as *being brought up to minimum standards.* At the meeting, recipients talked about never owning spatulas, measuring spoons, blankets, or adequate clothing. Discussions led to a desire to confront the department about minimum standard funds—a big step coming from people who never considered standing up to the department about anything. Now, bolstered by the knowledge that the influence and power of the Catholic church was behind them, the recipients prepared for action. Father Stevens fueled their resolve by distributing minimum standard forms. These forms listed every item a family should own, and how many—from socks and underwear to curtains and sheets. By the time the first meeting ended— as each of my respondents observed—

> I had begun to believe that welfare was a right, rather than a privilege; and that perhaps, acting collectively, we could bring about a change in the restrictive practices of the Department of Public Welfare.[19]

In subsequent months, this attitude placed recipients in conflict with the majority of society, since it is doubtful that Americans in general regarded welfare as a right. Mrs. Hanover explained to me that "Recipients felt comfortable at the meetings and their children were as welcome as they." Former recipients commented that — finally — they had found a group that centered on their specific concerns.

The enthusiasm of that first meeting extended to subsequent gatherings, and soon there were so many people attending that it was standing room only. In addition, word about the recipients' group spread through the community of priests. Father Matthews, a friend of Father Stevens, was one of those who became interested in this work. He subsequently teamed with Father Stevens to organize WROs. Hearing the clergymen criticize the institution so central to the recipients' existence was a vital organizing tool. As a result, the welfare system appeared less powerful — even vulnerable. Moreover, the recipients' complaints were being legitimized by the church.

Preparing for the First Demonstration

Father Stevens also described the different treatment that suburban or more affluent people were accustomed to receiving at the welfare centers in their areas. Caseworkers served those applicants in a respectful manner, and clients maintained their dignity. Suburbanites on welfare often received larger grants than inner-city residents of equal size families. Welfare policy at suburban centers was to fund clients at the level to which they were accustomed to living. For example, car payments (when used for work) or private school tuition were both included in the budget. Essentially, WRO members learned the meaning of being the undeserving poor from those lectures. The information made them sufficiently indignant and less fearful of organizing.

Recipients agreed to manage the storefront office when the nuns were absent or teaching. The simple act of volunteering added to new feelings of self-worth among the members. Their time was needed: They were as important as middle-class women who did volunteer work among the poor. They had taken another step toward empowering themselves and the community.

The volunteers' main responsibility was in compiling minimum standard forms (MSFs). Some MSFs were first distributed at the initial meeting; others were submitted to the storefront by people who had recently heard about its existence. The women reviewed these forms to determine whether they were complete and ready for presentation to the department. They answered phones and recruited interested recipients for future meetings.

Two weeks after the first session, Father Stevens and 25 welfare recipients delivered 25 MSFs to officials at the Livingston Welfare Center in downtown Brooklyn, and demanded that checks to purchase the items be ready the next day. Normally, such requests would have been refused; or, if they had been approved, three or four weeks would have elapsed before the funds arrived. But these checks were waiting when the group returned, much to their surprise. The women had expected to begin a long, hard battle to obtain the grants. Instead, they each received about $100 – a successful completion of their first welfare rights demonstration. They had acted in solidarity and won. The principals learned a major organizing lesson: An early success is necessary to retain interest and to enhance the recruitment program.

Things moved quickly after that. More welfare recipients – almost all women – visited the storefront office as word of the victory spread. At the same time, the nuns deliberately became less and less involved in the daily operations of the center. Within three months, welfare recipients were in charge of the storefront's operations and were fast becoming experts in assisting their peers by completing forms, accompanying people to the welfare centers, and even making referrals to other community service programs. The nuns remained available for consultations. Having reached across religious, class, and racial lines, they had helped a number of women begin the long trek to a better life.

About two years after organizing the welfare recipients of Bedford Stuyvesant, Sisters Tina, Joan, and Ruth left their order and moved to Milwaukee to teach and organize there. Before leaving, however, they witnessed a very important development. In May 1966, the recipient activists voted to establish a formal welfare rights group, naming their storefront the Neighborhood Action Center (NAC). This was the forerunner of 48 centers organized under the auspices of Fathers Stevens and Matthews. The members held elections that produced NAC's first officers. Its president was later to become the first chairperson of a boroughwide welfare rights union.

Fellow activists with whom I spoke maintained that the three church women were exemplary individuals, and well deserving of plaudits for their organizing feats. A more detailed examination of the clergy's lives and of the church's role in the welfare rights movement will shed further light on the purpose of the clergy's activism, as well as on the people they organized.

THE CATHOLIC CHURCH AND SOCIAL CHANGE

Many of Brooklyn's Catholic nuns and priests — imbued with the potential and promises of Vatican II[20] — believed that service to low-income people included sharing their pain and helping them to meet their earthly needs. Feeling the apparent winds of change, the nuns of Our Lady of Victory interpreted the council's pronouncements literally and liberally. They expanded the manifestation of their religious commitments beyond teaching and food baskets. Instead, these church women enthusiastically spearheaded an organizing drive that was to have national impact. Planting the seeds from which a boroughwide council would emerge before too long, the nuns at first proceeded independently of the parish priests. But they knew that the noblest of endeavors would languish if they did not attend to the pragmatic concerns of teaching and operating a convent. Moreover, the nuns were mindful of the limitations on women in the church's hierarchy. Consequently, enlisting the participation and services of a priest in their parish was a logical strategy to adopt.

Convincing Father Stevens to assist in their organizing efforts was easy. He was a man looking for a cause, and he found one. Two years later — in 1968 — Fathers Stevens and Matthews (the latter having begun to focus on the welfare rights effort while also organizing tenants) quoted the Vatican on the priesthood in a proposal to broaden and adjust parish work. The proposal was not funded. In spite of that, the two priests practiced an expansion of their theological responsibilities by directly confronting issues faced by community people.

Fathers Stevens and Matthews had faith in and a respect for people's ability — regardless of race, class, or gender. That faith was important, because their organizing activities and ways of motivating others stemmed more from intuition than from experience. Neither of the priests had any formal training in the field. In fact, they acquired some organizing theory only after the WROs had become successful. In 1968, the two priests studied at Saul Alinsky's Chicago institute of the Industrial Areas Foundation (IAF) — after the storefronts were functioning with minimal assistance from the clergy.

Essentially, the Alinsky model provided poor people with "the only real source they might have had — their standing and organizational capacity, leading to mobilization, confrontation and negotiation,"[21] in order to increase their share in the distribution of wealth and to strengthen their voice in the process of decision-making. Alinsky believed that a local, self-reliant, and community-based organization was the only antidote against the rising specter of fascism (right or left), which Alinsky attributed to the trend of increasing political centralization. In Alinsky's view, there was nothing basically wrong with the economic system except the insensitivity of the political institutions to the people, who were excluded because of bureaucratization, centralization, corruption, and manipulation of information.[22] Whether Fathers Stevens and Matthews were advocates of everything that Alinsky espoused is unknown. But they followed most of his tenets.

Heightened Awareness of Institutional Oppression

Father Stevens and Father Matthews were 2 out of 20 grassroots activist priests (there were 100 in the Brooklyn diocese). However, the major interests and contributions of these two men were in welfare rights organizing. The remaining priests worked with tenants and with drug addicts, as well as on school issues — particularly, community control of that institution. The Brooklyn diocese hierarchy was much less enamored with the teachings of Vatican II's European theologians than were its young clergy. Reluctance and a slow, deliberate pace on the part of the diocese in affirming the priests' work fostered the notion that the church fathers were actually resistant to change. However, the young priests' discontent concerning their general failure to influence the church's direction eased somewhat when funds were allocated for their organizing activities. In 1969, funding for the welfare rights storefronts (by then, there were 46) had reached nearly $700,000, from an initial grant of $14,000 to NAC (in 1967) for administration and recruitment purposes.[23]

Fathers Matthews and Stevens welcomed the financial support, but were unimpressed with its size. They maintained that such a rich institution could afford to contribute far more. Conversely — being rather thoroughly antiestablishment at this point — the two priests worried that diocesan largess might contain a different agenda, either to quiet them or to take the storefronts' control away from the members. In fact, their fears were eventually realized. Two years later — in 1971 — the Brooklyn diocese effectuated its control by replacing the indigenous staff with professional administrators and renaming the storefronts the Catholic Charities Human Resource Centers. (In Chapter 5, I have included a detailed on-site description of the measures taken by the diocese to engineer this change, as told by a recipient.)

Although the priests remained suspicious of its goals, Catholic Charities' funds had a great impact on the members' psyche, apart from the material aspects. Naturally, the acquisition of furniture, a telephone account, or rent for a newly organized storefront was appreciated by the activists. But also, the feeling of security — a connection to influential people — advanced a sense of invincibility. WRO participants observed that, whether at the welfare centers or at conferences, Brooklyn members invited attention and admiration because of their proud bearing and self-confidence.

The priests had not recognized the depth of clients' need for public backing and the acceptance of a powerful institution. Initially, they were puzzled and somewhat disdainful of members' reactions to the grant. Eventually, they came to understand the importance of the church's gift from the clients' viewpoint. In doing so, the priests learned three things: the extent to which politically unaware poor people feel shut out of the system; how much any show of kindness toward them is appreciated; and that rejection of a gift — or skepticism of a respected institution's motives — is a middle- and upper-class luxury.

Fathers Stevens and Matthews attempted to spread the gospel by sharing the lives of grant-income people, helping to inculcate in them a sense of self-worth, and prodding church officials to implement Vatican II's proposed changes — all of which were formidable challenges. They succeeded on the first two accounts. As explained in a 1979 report,

> The convergence of a newly emergent structure of consciousness and changing forces led to the development of this poverty movement. . . . Emphasis went from the church as a rigid authoritarian institution with

obedience as a prime virtue to the church as a community with agape — charity as the primary characteristic.[24]

To fulfill their mission, Fathers Stevens and Matthews petitioned the diocese in 1967 for permission to move out of the rectory and in to a nearby apartment. In their proposal, they stated that

The conditions of housing, ecumenism, education, youth, welfare and employment offer the church the opportunity of communicating the love of Christ in a meaningful way.

Having received the church's permission to live in an apartment — and as adherents of the post–World War II worker-priests movement in France[25] — the two clergymen embraced the life-style of the community. They began to see themselves as

Street people and to dress and behave accordingly. [They wore] the uniform of community workers: desert boots, chinos, work shirts, surplus army jackets and berets; their language became much more that of the "street." [They were] with the people more than with clerical friends and it became quite common to find the priests at local social functions and parties.[26]

Fathers Matthews and Stevens became so well known that a local newspaper did a feature article on their activities. In time, their association with the poor and disadvantaged earned them the nickname "ghetto priests." Under their auspices, 15 additional storefront centers were established — primarily in Bedford Stuyvesant, which was essentially an African-American neighborhood. All the storefronts' names were similar to each other — Fulton Action Center (FAC), Broadway Action Center (BAC), and Grand Action Center (GAC), for instance — but NAC remained the flagship of welfare rights in Brooklyn.

The era of community action on the part of nonblacks ended abruptly in 1968 — more quickly than one would have thought possible — partly because of ghetto uprisings. After Dr. Martin Luther King, Jr.'s assassination in April 1968, Father Matthews commented that his white skin had become a liability. In response to this situation, he submitted a proposal to the diocese in 1969 for the establishment of a comparable experimental ministry in the white community. To what extent Dr. King's death galvanized Father Matthews into acting thus is not clear. But in the proposal — which did not receive funds — he commented,

> It has often been said that we have not a black problem, but a white one. The problems of Bed-Stuy and Bayside are not so different. Each community interacts and influences the other; in some cases there is even a causal relationship.

The priests had been experiencing problems with church officials. Their new thinking and posture made them impatient with the church's slow, methodical approach to community action. Fathers Stevens and Matthews perceived little or no desire within the hierarchy to respond quickly to the plight of the poor. Father Matthews, who had studied in Paris and had firsthand knowledge of the worker-priests movement, was particularly restless. He and Stevens believed that Vatican II and Pope John XXIII had intended for the Roman Catholic church to move away from lavish appointments and splendor, to caring for the poor and powerless. As noted above, "Emphasis went from the church as a rigid authoritarian institution . . . to the church as a community."[27] Most of the advocate clergy believed that they were faced with an essentially unsympathetic church leadership in the Brooklyn diocese. They saw their gains slowly eroding as political and ecclesiastical conservatism began to reassert itself. Disillusioned by the church's unresponsiveness and for other personal reasons, Father Matthews left the priesthood in 1968. Father Stevens remained a year longer, trying unsuccessfully to organize men of color; but then he, too, left the cloth.

They were not alone. From 1966–70, the post–Vatican II years during which the advocate clergy was most active, the Roman Catholic church in the United States, and the Brooklyn diocese specifically, suffered a large exodus of priests and nuns due in part to a reexamining of vows that left the dissenters unhappy with the church's direction and approach to poverty issues. The church has not yet recovered from that experience, and the number of priests and nuns continues to dwindle. One priest who stayed, Father Johnston, commented,

> The church was involved because of dynamic, dedicated priests who were committed to serving the people in their community and training them to regain control of their lives. What the real contribution was that the Diocese let the religious people to do what they wanted; it didn't interfere. The 60's was a unique time, [and we] won't see a replay. It was an exciting beautiful, challenging time.[28]

LACK OF BLACK CLERGY AND MIDDLE-CLASS INVOLVEMENT

There was a bewildering phenomenon happening here: Why did all this activity in Brooklyn fail to attract resources and clergy from African-American and Caribbean religious institutions? Traditionally, the African-American church — at least the southern component — had been the natural organizer in the African-American community. It had assumed the leadership role in the 1960s' civil-rights southern campaign. However, the welfare rights arena, was virtually devoid of any African-American and Caribbean clergy or middle-class participation. I asked every person I interviewed why this had occurred. One respondent, who was a civil rights activist, commented that

> The black church's position or refusal to help is not surprising; northern churches haven't been active on the

grass roots level in forty years. They don't live or invest in
the community. . . . Northern black religious institutions
are middle class and out of touch.[29]

The Catholic clergy and theorists with whom I spoke pointed
out that black ministers often had to augment their income with
daily employment, and thus were unavailable to organize the
poor. Client respondents believed that classism was the reason
for the absence of the black middle class, who — according to
my interviewees — were ashamed of the welfare rights activities. Pentecostal clergy were the exception. Two Pentecostal
ministers in the Bedford Stuyvesant community were sympathetic, and sometimes helpful. In one instance, welfare rights
members received permission to address their congregations
on Mother's Day in 1968. The women's purpose was to ac-
quaint the congregations with WRO and the inequities of the
welfare system. Participants hoped that their message would
reach unaffiliated welfare recipients who were still too afraid
to come out of the closet. Lastly, WRO people assumed that
this recruiting strategy would generate black middle-class
friends for welfare rights.

But the maneuver went untried on any large scale because,
although WRO members met with several Baptist and Methodist
clergy of the largest congregations in Brooklyn, not one of them
granted their request to speak. Even leafleting was denied; the
ministers limited WRO members to the sidewalks across the
street from their churches. To ignore that instruction would have
put the clients in jeopardy of arrest. Perhaps the activities of the
organized welfare clients embarrassed the African-American
clergy and middle class. Or should we attribute their unsympathetic stance to the fact that this was a women's movement, and
therefore of no real consequence? Yet weren't the majority of the
congregations female — particularly the most active members? In
fact, were not a number of parishioners receiving welfare? When
asked about these issues during my interviews, Catholic clergy
members observed that the African-American clergy had not
been invited to join the movement in Brooklyn.

This point is well taken, since the Reverend Mr. Simpson of a Baptist church in Brooklyn told me that "Black theologians were not actively solicitated for the welfare rights movement."[30] Nonetheless, the late George Wiley, executive director of the national office of NWRO, did receive some financial support from Brooklyn ministers. Thus, the welfare fair-rights campaign was known to the African-American clergy people. Moreover, a division of Brooklyn's Operation Breadbasket (a community action organization with headquarters in Chicago) had a welfare rights section, as the Reverend Mr. Simpson noted. When queried as to whether the African-American and Caribbean middle class harbored any shame or embarrassment about welfare rights activities, Simpson responded ambiguously, commenting that the media promoted negative feelings about recipients of public assistance. He pointed out that the government was responsible for providing assistance to citizens "not gainfully employed."

If African-American church men and women were — typically — less than knowledgeable about the needs and concerns of the poor, then the same thinking must have extended to the other middle-class African-American institutions that also ignored the organized clients' efforts. In any case, the African-American church was conspicuously absent in Brooklyn's welfare rights movement.

On the other hand, the number of welfare rights supporters did increase, including the Brooklyn Congress of Racial Equality (CORE) — which joined welfare rights actions and attended fundraising events — and the Brooklyn Black Panther party. The latter organization volunteered as marshals and guards at demonstrations after local police initiated violence against the women and children. In 1968 when the Southern Christian Leadership Conference (SCLC) needed people for the White House–lawn encampment of poor people (tent city), it approached welfare rights leaders about enlisting members' participation. Some WRO people did participate, but that was essentially the extent of SCLC's involvement with welfare rights.

Two civil rights activists—Dick Gregory and the late Fannie Lou Hamer—were among the few people with national stature to address WRO conferences and attend meetings. Mr. Gregory summarized the conditions of grant-income people for those individuals chagrined by noisy demands for more money:

> I am sick and tired of having to apologize for the acceptance of public aid by needy people. It is in the public interest, especially under the capitalist system, to raise the living standard of the lowest to a position where it can afford to enter the marketplace. It was on this principle that the United States rebuilt Germany and Japan and established the Marshall Plan. Farmers regularly receive federal subsistence. The airlines are financed by federal subsidy. The railroads continue to exist because of federal grants. Great oil companies receive enormous tax allowances; and yet, somehow poor families without employment must apologize for receiving public aid. What's needed is improved services along with increased and realistic allowances; vocational training and expanding job opportunity (including the end of union discrimination) to enable the recipient to help himself [or herself] into a place of independent productivity.[31]

SOME PROGRESS IN THE STRUGGLE FOR DIGNITY

Women on welfare joined welfare rights groups by the hundreds. They attended meetings that covered and detailed their entitlement under state social-service laws. Money was the initial incentive; and the women discovered that, while they were struggling with meager budgets, the Welfare Department was denying them access to millions of dollars. Those who remained with the movement believed that they could promote a higher standard of living for everyone. At the other end of the spectrum were the department staff, who felt powerless—in such a large bureaucracy—to provide adequate services. Most staff knew little about available entitlement for clients. One caseworker said that massive paperwork and endless signatures were a barrier against issuing special grants. Clients discovered that these funds were still available. Anger over this revelation motivated them to organize and share the information with others. Accordingly, they ascertained that group action would free the money from bureaucratic constraints—that maneuver resulted in the release of checks for clothing and furniture.

The development of a strategy regarding the disputed funds' release warrants further description. When the first welfare rights organization (NAC) was established in Brooklyn, between 25 and 50 forms were submitted once a week to the department by a representative member, with a like number of recipients in attendance. Each newly issued welfare grant was displayed and loudly discussed by the welfare rights organizers, sometimes followed up with testimonials by new members. Immediately, 20 or 30 people would inquire about welfare rights membership. Often, every client in a center would join; the numbers ranged from 20 to 100 depending on how many people were present.

WRO's wholesale on-site recruiting disturbed the department officials. They countered by releasing organized members' checks as quickly as possible, thereby clearing the premises of welfare rights activists. Organizers met that challenge by developing a different recruitment plan. WRO participants set up tables outside every welfare office, providing information along with membership applications and referrals to other agencies and welfare rights groups in the client's residential area. As vital as this undertaking was, staffing the tables added a real burden to the organized recipients' heavy schedule—which included client representation at schools, clinics, court, and other welfare centers. In addition, participants had to maintain their distribution of information about the movement and welfare entitlements in the neighborhoods, at housing projects, drug rehabilitation centers, grocery stores, Head Start nurseries, and food distribution centers, as well as schools. Eventually, they had to discontinue staffing the recruitment tables, having spread themselves too thin.

To the WRO members' credit, the Welfare Department adopted the information-table concept citywide. However, unorganized clients who had close ties and loyalties to the department staffed the tables, and recipients received almost no information about the welfare rights movement.

Organized members discovered that the department's stance concerning the withholding of special grants extended to other areas as well. These policies were contributors to reducing the quality of life for people receiving welfare. WRO's demands for financial remuneration were unremitting. Concurrently, service with dignity and respect assumed new importance and was viewed as a basic right.

Brooklyn welfare rights organizers instituted efforts to improve caseworkers' behavior and attitudes toward clients. They stressed that, theoretically, the clients were the bosses of the caseworkers and should be treated accordingly. For instance, Mary Gantry would respond to department staff only when addressed as Ms. Gantry. And Ms. Gantry demanded a quiet place—with a chair—for meetings with her caseworker.

On another front, unannounced home visits by welfare staff were no longer tolerated. In 1968, welfare rights groups negotiated an agreement with the department, ending the caseworker's practice of visiting a client's home without an appointment. Nor were caseworkers permitted to search clients' homes—including trunks, closets, dressers, or under the beds. Staff had justified this activity as an attempt to determine whether a man was living with the ADC client. The most extreme form of this practice manifested itself in the midnight raid, when caseworkers would arrive late at night to search for a man sleeping in their client's house. This was such a loathsome and potentially violent practice for everyone concerned that Mitchell Ginsberg's first official order on being appointed welfare commissioner in 1966 was to end it. In 1968, a caseworker who was speaking in support of home visits without appointments said,

> Our powers of investigation have been so severely limited that almost anything goes now. The situation has gotten completely out of hand. We are far from home breakers.[32]

Questioning clients' children about visitors was another problem that ceased — as did inquiries regarding when, where, and by whom a client had become pregnant. In sum, many daily indignities were eliminated, due primarily to the welfare rights organizations' efforts and a relatively progressive city administration.

A DEPARTMENT-FUNDED COMMUNITY RELATIONS UNIT

Commissioner Ginsberg introduced another variable into the department's changing consciousness. Welfare department employees were assigned as community organizers (COs). These staff members worked out of the newly formed community relations section of the department with these mandates: to keep welfare centers open and functioning, to head off demonstrations or at least make certain that the actions were violence free, and to work toward limiting confrontations between staff and organized recipients. Also, the COs had instructions to cultivate and maintain close ties with welfare rights groups as well as establish the Welfare Department's Client Advisory Committees (CACs).[33]

Reporting to their community relations supervisor at the department's central office in Manhattan — and with direct access to Ginsberg when necessary — the COs had the power to override local department supervisors' decisions. They could and did authorize the release of checks, approve apartments, and stop evictions by assuring the landlord that a rent check would arrive at a specific date — sometimes over the objections of department colleagues. COs would stay for the duration of any demonstration, often defusing confrontations and preventing the city or the department from ordering police arrests.

Recognizing the COs' positive manner and approach to problems encountered by clients, the WROs accepted them essentially as Welfare Department staff who were sympathetic and concerned about recipients, but who were still the enemy. Department staff knew and respected the members' posture. Conversely, COs kept their own objectives foremost, being mindful of where the WROs' and their own loyalties lay. Both groups had diverse yet occasionally parallel goals. To meet them — explained one CO — the two groups used one another.

In 1983 (at different locations and times), I interviewed two male former COs — one black and one white — who reaffirmed the above sentiments, and even agreed that the welfare rights movement furthered the cause of recipients. Each commented that client needs and concerns had been thrust onto the public stage by the WROs, encouraging city and national officials to think about the issues and possible solutions. As one of them said,

> WROs were effective, clients did receive more money than they would have gotten [on their own], the same was true for services; also they were effective in changing policies and procedures in the individual centers. Finally they [the WROs] addressed or changed the attitude of caseworkers [toward the client].[34]

The other CO noted that

> Caseworkers were aware of the [department's] injustices, but were also intimidated and fearful of clients; in addition they didn't want to be bothered filling out zillions of forms to give people what they were entitled to.[35]

Often the COs' and the clients' interests would merge: The COs needed peace in the centers, and the clients wanted all the benefits to which they were legally entitled. Caseworkers held the key to the welfare-office peace, by facilitating service and denying or approving grant requests.

Since most caseworkers did not know what the client was entitled to, disputes and problems were commonplace. Rules and regulations were numerous, confusing, contradictory, and subject to frequent changes. In addition,

> The union [SSEU] was not as supportive [of clients] as it should have been. It should have issued directives to CWs [caseworkers] that clients should get everything they were entitled to. The union's only memorandum about WROs' protests was the issue of getting paid for overtime when WRO kept the [welfare] centers open [past five o'clock].[36]

So we see that the COs I interviewed were critical of the department and knew that clients were being treated unfairly. They acknowledged that this view had changed since the time when they first arrived at the Welfare Department. In 1966, COs considered themselves politically radical, which symbolized New York City's new climate of improving services for its constituents. Yet, each of the two men admitted wondering why recipients "didn't pick themselves up by their bootstraps and go to work." Try as they might, they could not rid themselves of that notion, in spite of the pain and suffering they saw daily.

Both of these COs had been born in New York City, and were products of a working-class background. They attended college, and then obtained master degrees in social work — tuition free — at the City University while they were employees of the Welfare Department. The privilege of pursuing a degree was a powerful incentive to join the department. As one of the COs noted, white working-class youths were its chief beneficiaries. Both acknowledged that — at the time — neither realized that they too were receiving a form of public assistance. "Perhaps because it was provided without any stigma attached, one does not associate college grants and assistance with welfare payments," he said. Their salary continued while they were in college, as did their promotions.

In 1983, these two men considered themselves progressives but espoused "conservative" ideas. "Perhaps radicalism is for youth" was their attitude. The quote that follows—by CO Halprin—echoes the sentiment of the establishment professional males (with the notable exception of Ginsberg, the former welfare commissioner) interviewed during this research:

Ending poverty, discrimination and racism in this country is a very complex assignment; besides there's been a lot of progress in employment, housing and electoral politics. Look at me: I'm the first in my family to go to college; my parents were immigrants with no academic credentials. My mother even stood in line for surplus food (my father refused to go). Me and my family paid our dues.[37]

Stated another way, the former CO is implying that, since he advanced, recipients should also be able to help themselves. During the peak of welfare rights actions, the COs worked long hours to keep the bureaucracy functioning. Their favored status at the department's central office resulted from the commissioner's dependence on them to prevent or eliminate conflict in the local centers. An orderly Welfare Department was necessary for making changes, according to Commissioner Ginsberg. Having expended a great deal of time and energy pushing for welfare reform at the local and national levels, Ginsberg was now eager to implement his ideas using the widespread resources of HRA—one of the largest service institutions in the nation.

Establishing a community relations unit was a relatively minor—although important—initiative when compared with his other, more long-range efforts, since clients' short-term needs were the new unit's focus. Ginsberg made a revolutionary change in 1968 when he instituted an experimental simplification of applications, known as "a declaration of need." Clients signed a simple form declaring their need for financial assistance. They were given funds on the same day.[38]

Ginsberg faced strong opposition to that program and to others that he sought to establish. The simplification of all applications, increased benefits, food stamps, the institutionalization of client advisory groups, and a federally administered welfare program were on his agenda. He was true to his reputation as being sympathetic to the needs of poor people. Having arrived with progressive credentials, he could count several citywide WRO leaders among his friends.

Characteristically, Brooklyn members and WRO officers decided against being friendly or associating with any Welfare Department heads, regardless of their progressive stance. Brooklyn WRO leaders remained suspicious of officialdom and ever mindful that members could very well misconstrue innocent associations or—which was more important—be offended by such friendships. A cordial and professional yet aloof manner was assumed and followed by most members in Brooklyn. WRO participants were taught that the acquisition of human rights, dignity, and justice was best accomplished by organizing persons currently shut out of the system. And this would be made easier by limiting social exchanges between employees of the establishment and themselves.

Organized clients believed that clearly drawn ideological battle lines fostered a distinct sense of purpose and goals in the struggle for rights. In WRO members' judgment, people on the establishment's payroll—whether well intentioned or not—were part of the problem, and not the solution. To leave the institutions and promote the interests of poor people was a stance that spoke louder than any compassionate statements. Nonetheless, had they looked carefully at the future, participants might have responded differently to this situation, since hard times were on the horizon and WRO would need friends inside the bureaucracies.

With the exception of the summer of 1968, Brooklyn's achievements and activities attracted less ongoing publicity than activism in other boroughs, particularly since reporters were considered the enemy along with most unionists, social workers, Catholic Charities officials, and even NWRO staff and officers at one time or another. This attitude must have stemmed from Father Stevens, who was suspicious of "outsiders"—especially politicians. Scorning assistance from people outside the borough, Brooklyn members were self-contained with the Catholic church's financial and spiritual support. Such an isolationist posture contradicted the notion of unity among all recipients, and we shall see that this aloofness was one of B-WAC's weaknesses. "Welfare rights organizations across the country deplored what they perceived to be Brooklyn's arrogance, but admired its innovativeness and thoroughness," observed an organizer. NWRO adopted many Brooklyn initiatives, such as member and leadership training classes. In fact, the drive to obtain financial credit terms for people on welfare—began in Brooklyn and spread around the country. It culminated in 1969 with an unsuccessful national campaign aimed at forcing Sears, Roebuck and Co. to extend credit to grant-income people.[39]

Thus, Brooklyn's self-imposed isolation lessened the opportunity for recognition of its creativity and its pioneering efforts to remove barriers in all social and economic areas affecting welfare recipients' lives. Local politicians—a very important mainstream group—were well aware of organized clients and their strengths. A few elected officials visited storefronts and met with the client leaders. Their chief goal was to secure political endorsements. Instead, what these politicians met was a refusal on the part of an important community and borough organization to endorse or campaign for any candidate. Hindsight shows that plans should have been developed and implemented to move into electoral politics. With Brooklyn so tightly organized, political activity had real potential. Groups similar to B-WAC around the nation could have made the difference at some elections. When Cloward and Piven called for a massive voter education and registration campaign 16 years later in 1984, they would have encountered fewer difficulties and would have been more successful if more grass roots institutions had been in existence. Yet Cloward and Piven remain opposed to the fostering of dues-paying poor people's organizations.

Some individual members did volunteer their time during the 1968 electoral campaigns, and helped alert the community to office seekers with proven concern about recipients and poor people in general. In fact, WRO initiated a successful nonpartisan voter education/registration drive as well as helped many people to vote for the first time by sending client representatives to take them to polling places or provide babysitting services.

Voter education and registration was one additional factor in the recipients' process of taking control of their lives. From "low self-esteem as well as a sense of hopelessness" — observed a respondent — to organization, negotiation, and political awakening. WRO members had made visible progress. At this juncture I shall back up in order to examine in detail the clients' initial confrontations with the Welfare Department.

NOTES

1. CORE refers to the Congress of Racial Equality. George Wiley later became the executive director of NWRO.

2. Richard Cloward and Frances Fox Piven, "A Strategy to End Poverty," *Nation*, May 2, 1966.

3. Marcia Guttentag, "Group Cohesiveness: Ethnic Organization and Poverty," *Journal of Social Issues* 26, 2 (Spring 1970): 124–28. (I support the organizers' view that poor people can obtain a measure of power and change through collective action within a formal organization.)

4. See Richard Cloward and Frances Fox Piven, *Poor People's Movements: Why They Succeed, How They Fail* (New York: Vintage Books, 1979), p. 296.

5. Norman Fainstein and Susan Fainstein, *Urban Political Movements* (Englewood Cliffs, N.J.: Prentice-Hall, 1974), p. 197: "Bureaucratic personnel are often unaccustomed to stressful situations."

6. See Larry Jackson and William Johnson, *Protest by the Poor: The Welfare Rights Movement in New York City* (New York: Rand Corporation, 1973).

7. New York City Department of Welfare, *Monthly Statistical Reports*,

January 1966 and 1969.

8. New York City Department of Welfare, *Monthly Statistical Reports*, June, July, and August 1963 and 1968. See Table IV for total grants citywide.

9. Cloward's statement—made during an interview in the fall of 1983 at the Columbia School of Social Work—raises several questions: Does this mean that people on welfare do not warrant organizing? Would welfare clients have any leadership role in the new coalition of people (not groups or organizations, says Cloward)? These questions remain unanswered. But Cloward seems to believe that people on welfare who are organized without support from the larger community would hardly be able to reach their goals.

10. Ibid.

11. Ibid.

12. The nuns were apostolates in the Sisters of St. Joseph order, which in 1966 numbered about 2,000 nationally. Seventeen of them taught at Our Lady of Victory School in Brooklyn's Bedford Stuyvesant neighborhood. At its peak the school's enrollment—grades 1–8—numbered 700 students, primarily African-American and African-Caribbean children. The school was a religiously mixed institution, but predominantly Catholic. The average age of the nuns was 25.

13. Mailboxes were regularly burglarized in low-income neighborhoods; stolen checks were a recurring problem, according to interviewees. Further, there were instances where people lost all benefits because they failed to respond to a Welfare Department letter or notice that had never been received.

14. This was a private survey conducted by the group of nuns at Our Lady of Victory School, and was not made public—nor is it presently available.

15. From the author's May 1983 interview with two of the former clergywomen, which included a discussion of the neighborhood survey.

16. Ibid.

17. The storefront's address was 699 Gates Avenue, Brooklyn, New York.

18. This was also a private survey conducted by the nuns; it is not available.

19. Statements and descriptions here are from my interviews with former client activists in the summers of 1982 and 1983 in Brooklyn and Manhattan, New York City.

20. Vatican II was a council of the Roman Catholic church's highest officials convened in Rome in 1962 by Pope John XXIII to reestablish and modernize religious guidelines for its clergy and laypeople.

21. Manuel Castells, *The City and the Grass Roots* (Berkeley: University

of California Press, 1983), p. 139.

22. Ibid.

23. Precise figures are unavailable. Father Robert Kennedy, the priest who handled welfare-rights organizing expenses at the Brooklyn diocese, died in 1982 four days prior to a scheduled interview with this author. I gather from subsequent interviews with Bishops Joseph Sullivan and Frances Mc-Guvero that Father Kennedy kept few records of the 1960s activities. Church officials have indicated that he operated with minimal supervision. Presumably, if any records were kept, they have since been discarded. However, John R. Sullivan – Father Kennedy's former assistant and a former priest – agreed with the guesstimates that I have quoted from Father Stevens. Unfortunately, Sullivan too had no records.

24. Unpublished mimeographed report by John Hylan and James Regan, "Poverty Movement: Medieval Europe and Brooklyn, 1960–1970," 1979.

25. The Little Brothers of Jesus – founded by a Frenchman, Father René Voillaume – lived and worked among the poorest people in groups of twos and threes, "sharing their poverty and struggles." See Hyland and Regan, "Poverty Movement."

26. Ibid.

27. For a discussion of the radical church's responsibilities, see ibid.

28. From the author's March 1983 interview with Father Johnston in Brooklyn, New York.

29. From an interview by the author in Brooklyn, New York, in August 1983. All former clients and staff voiced similar – and even stronger – negative views about the black churches' absence in the WRO movement.

30. From the author's 1985 telephone interview with the Reverend Mr. Simpson in Brooklyn, New York.

31. *NOW! The National Welfare Leaders Newsletter* 2, 13 (October 1968): 8.

32. Name withheld, "Many on Welfare Are Needy, Caseworker Says, But Not All," *Tablet*, April 28, 1968, p. 12.

33. The CACs were the Welfare Department's answer to organized clients. Picked by caseworkers throughout the city, most of these recipients were politically uninformed. While some feared that their cases would be closed if they refused the appointment, others gladly agreed to serve because – as noted by the COs – they viewed themselves as being better than the average client. Unaffiliated recipients were confused by the existence of two client groups. This became a divisive tactic, pitting so-called upper-class recipients against the rabble-rousers in a situation similar to company unions versus people's unions.

34. From separate interviews by the author in the summer of 1983 at

offices in New York City.

35. Ibid.

36. Ibid.

37. Quotations and other comments here are from separate interviews by the author at different locations in New York City in the summer of 1983 and the fall of 1984.

38. Every tenth client was thoroughly investigated, and about 2 percent were deemed ineligible. Caseworker time was better utilized since investigative tasks were almost eliminated. Therefore the city saved money. However, the changing political climate forced the procedure's discontinuance in 1969.

39. For a substantive description of these programs and mobilization activities, see Chapter 5.

4

Organized Recipients Begin Challenging Social Institutions

Literature on European born women refers to their courage and strength when faced with rearing their families alone.... Black women, who because of racial discrimination require more strength to cope with life alone, are often the recipients of harsh criticism and negative labels. Unmotivated, lazy and immoral are adjectives frequently applied to black women forced to accept public assistance.[1]

Middle-class people of color as well as welfare recipients themselves have accepted these negative concepts, since nearly everyone believes in the Protestant work ethic. The creed of survival of the fittest, which is accepted by so many Americans, exacerbates the problem. Women receiving public assistance are neither fit nor — according to the larger society — believers in the work ethic. Their work as parents has been undervalued or ignored entirely. Yet, should caring for her children render a welfare mother mentally and physically helpless, the city/state then hires a housekeeper or foster parent to assume the child-rearing responsibility at a relatively handsome salary. In any case, being unemployed single parents has isolated these women still more. Accordingly, their needs have been alternately discovered and forgotten again and again by academics, political activists, and the general public.

In the 1960s, Daniel Moynihan focused on the low-income black family in his book *The Negro Family : A Case for National Action*:

> At the heart of the deterioration of the fabric of Negro society is the deterioration of the Negro family. This is the fundamental source of the weakness of the Negro community at the present time.[2]

Unpropitiously, many academicians and the black community initially accepted this report's findings wholesale. Some time later, more thoughtful people recognized its limitations and launched a campaign to counter the report's influence. Moynihan was in effect blaming the victims for what was actually their strength and fortitude in withstanding adversity. In addition to social ostracism of their family circumstances, black recipients of public assistance had to contend with racial, gender, age, and class prejudices. It was to counter the effects of these issues that they joined NAC—an organization that respected them as adults and offered them the opportunity for action to secure their rights from the Welfare Department.

With the Catholic clergy's assistance, the organized recipients of Brooklyn matured both intellectually and politically. Encouraged to go past previous limits, the members discovered skills that they did not know they had. They used the planning of agendas and demonstrations and their scheduling of and participation in meetings with welfare and other city officials as strategies to remove previous insecurities and develop self-confidence, pride, and dignity. NAC—the ramshackle storefront that was their base of operation—often remained open past 11 o'clock at night when members were holding a sit-in at a welfare office, or when activists were conducting a postdemonstration analysis. The usual duration of these analysis sessions was a minimum of three hours. Thus, NAC's lights were on—and the doors open, in warm weather—

into the morning's early hours.

When mothers were at demonstrations or meetings, their children were cared for by other members: Everyone had some task. Nondemonstrators provided hot meals for the children, helped them with homework, and bedded them down at the adult's own home or the child's, as well as washed and ironed the next day's school clothes, if necessary. Additional support members prepared and delivered meals to those at the welfare office. Others alerted the press, and located and dispatched volunteer lawyers to the demonstration site if arrests were the group's objective for that particular action—or in the event of unanticipated jailings.

Shifts of reinforcements were regularly sent to demonstration sites often simply to bolster morale, or else to join the action. Participating in a demonstration was one assignment that was eagerly sought, since being in the public eye provided a certain degree of glamour for the members. However, a number of women could not join the demonstrators because of serious health problems, so they were part of the support group performing various in-house tasks and coordinating efforts.

Just as review sessions were conducted after every action, the same held true for meetings with agencies or government officials. Constructive criticism was encouraged, even from those who had not attended the meeting or sit-in. All the comments were well received because, in truth, the gatherings were political awareness sessions. Members were learning how and why they and other Americans were often victimized by the political and welfare processes. A sense of who gained from these systems was also acquired. NAC's strength lay in its ability to involve everyone in the group's activities, promote a sense of belonging, and instill confidence into its members. They discovered that the local directors were administering each welfare office as a fiefdom, that policies varied from center to center, and that laws were ignored or enforced at each director's discretion.

The NAC activists responded to this discovery by assigning

participants to specific centers, which enabled them to be familiar with that center's policies. These advocates absorbed the policy information well and soon acquired a reputation for mental acuity.

INCREASED UNITY AND UNDERSTANDING AMONG RECIPIENTS

Welfare rights advocates had one motto: the client is always right. With that principle as the advocate's guide, even clients with unsavory reputations or those discovered to be less than candid with the facts received strong support and assistance in the caseworker's presence. One former client compared the situation with the honor code among police, doctors, and other professionals. But in the case of NAC, members either soundly reprimanded these miscreant types afterward, or assumed the posture that future assistance from the WRO center would be refused. Such actions were necessary to safeguard the reputation of NAC and to avoid a lawsuit for complicity in fraud.

Admittedly, their strict holding to that stance caused some problems for NAC members. There were times when clients would become so incensed that they would physically threaten WRO representatives. Normally, other members were available to offer assistance. There were also times when pressure was exerted by the Welfare Department staff on the advocates, who themselves were receiving public assistance. This might include delayed checks and case closings. In each situation, NAC members banded together and won. They warned that centers would be closed by sit-ins unless the department ceased its activities against a welfare rights representative or member. Rarely did they need to carry out this threat since it was general knowledge that NAC could mobilize more than 200 demonstrators on short notice.

NAC members had acquired the expertise to obtain results. On any given day, representatives and clients would arrive at the department with completed minimum standard forms for processing. By encouraging every one of its members to stay until all the checks were distributed, NAC forced the social services staff to process its clients first. The longer the NAC representatives remained in the department's offices, the more unaffiliated welfare recipients would ask them for assistance — thereby expanding the ranks of organized clients. Sometimes every recipient in the center would designate the welfare rights advocates as their spokespersons. For this reason, the welfare centers often had to remain open past closing time and on into the night. Appointing a WRO member as representative was an important step for a client because "it signaled that he or she had begun to defy and question the system."[3]

Welfare rights advocates never volunteered to represent anyone. Even when the representative knew that someone's rights were being violated or that a person had received false information, she or he would not intervene unless a client specifically requested assistance. This posture fostered a respect for the client's wishes and acknowledged the person as a mature adult, able to make her or his own decisions. Advocates attempted to impart a sense of self-worth to all welfare clients. Therefore, NAC's confidence-building function also extended to nonmembers.

As NAC's advocacy role grew, it wasn't long before members were representing clients at fair hearing sessions, functioning as paralegal professionals in more complicated situations than were found at the local welfare centers. The fair hearing was a means of redress for recipients who had been denied requests for special services (like acupuncture) or items (a medically required bed with a motor, for example) that were not part of the normal budget. Activists' involvement ranged from lending moral support, to negotiating on a member's behalf when the client felt inadequately skilled to do so.

At the local centers, WRO participants helped clients with such problems as actual or pending evictions, approvals to move, and application denials. The activists might assist in obtaining an air conditioner for an asthmatic, a car for employment purposes, a college grant, or approval for cosmetic surgery (provided such requests related to job-seeking needs). Often the department would acquiesce in cases of alleged violations, because the advocates knew the regulations as well or better than the department staff did and because officials wanted to avoid demonstrations. Welfare staff actually made the advocacy roles of WRO members easier by engaging in violations of clients' rights, which ranged from underbudgeting to denial of special grants.

NAC gained additional strength because every welfare recipient was viewed as a potential advocate and was pressed into service soon after she joined. This was necessary because it was extremely difficult for the volunteers to maintain the hectic pace required to keep up with the welfare centers' operations. NAC's officers and members were also encouraged to move into other areas, such as public speaking, attending conferences and meetings, and expanding their organizational skills by networking with activists in other social change arenas. They were members of a support group that had been born of necessity, and these WRO activists had "graduated" to administering the cheapest and most effective on-the-job training program in the United States. WRO members acquired a variety of marketable skills — including clerical and administrative techniques, program planning and implementation, in addition to the ability to function in a team.

At the same time, recipients in general — not just WRO members — were making gains because of the welfare rights movement. From the *B-WAC Newsletter* dated January 29, 1969 — which was distributed all over the borough as well as at welfare centers in other parts of the city — one can see the full story emerging. Clients had seized the opportunity to learn and do things that financially secure Americans have always accepted as a given. In this supportive atmosphere, WRO members could fail without being rejected; in most instances, however, the women triumphed. Respondents in my study indicated that this encouragement and praise combined with modified applications of Cloward and Piven's welfare theory were the foundation of WRO success. Some organizers believed that the welfare rights movement even helped middle-class activists to become more action oriented regarding their own needs. Embarrassment about sitting-in was less of an issue. The movement for community control of all institutions — schools, hospitals, police and fire departments — gained new adherents, due in some degree to welfare recipients' speaking out about their problems. Civil rights activities in general had a significant impact on many sectors of society. The organizers with whom I spoke maintained that middle-class women, ethnic white Americans, and homosexuals were influenced by the movement and felt impelled to publicly respond to their own issues.

ATTEMPTS TO CHANGE OR ELIMINATE THE WELFARE SYSTEM

Brooklyn activists' goals included ending welfare dependency, improving the quality of life for low- and grant-income persons, and fostering dignity and self-respect. Their efforts encountered tremendous barriers. Activists have noted in retrospect that more consideration should have been given to eliminating the system, instead of attempting to change it. The welfare system in the 1960s was strong yet soft and flexible enough to resist efforts to restructure it. It employed a dual defense of implementing surface modifications and employing some of the key opposition leaders. Simultaneously, the welfare system's weaknesses invited attack, since — according to interviewees — its constituents were often emotionally less able to function after they received its services. An editorial in a Brooklyn newspaper criticized the welfare system thus:

> The best approach to the welfare system is not to reform it but to replace it with a new system that assures people in need an adequate income on an equitable basis.... This other American can no longer be ignored, despised and

rejected. The ultimate security of all Americans is dependent upon the success of our efforts to end poverty.[4]

Earlier that year, on February 22, 1969, an article appeared in another Brooklyn weekly that quoted Fred Salmon, chairman of New York Congressman Bertram Podell's Advisory Committee on Urban Development and Housing. Salmon announced that he favored national welfare standards, declaring that "the growing costs of welfare were playing havoc with both city and state budgets in New York."[5] He observed that the federal government would have to take action to ease this financial burden. The advisory committee was studying the entire welfare problem, including the proposal for a negative income tax as a replacement for welfare.

These articles illustrate the prevailing depth of feeling against the U.S. welfare system in the 1960s. Few people had kind words for it. Yet approaches to a solution so divided the population that substantive changes could not be effectuated. The system remained the same, and even possibly became more powerful. Indications are that department staff were dissatisfied with their positions and responsibilities in the bureaucracy. One caseworker interviewed in 1983 admitted feeling like "a pawn in some gigantic game in which no group could win." But others believed that the system's strengths were greater than its flaws and that minor adjustments would enable staff to function properly, hence providing better service to the constituents.

On the other side of the issue former activists were in consensus that the U.S. system of social welfare provides services and benefits to corporations in a humane and dignified manner. The subsidy system that distributes funds and other federal-government financial supports to businesses does function satisfactorily for its constituents. These businesses are dependent on the federal government's largess, while individuals who are public assistance recipients struggle against the dependency: The difference is that one group is indulged, and the other scorned for accepting handouts. Seldom are complaints heard from the business community about their treatment except when subsidies are reduced or eliminated. In 1982, Reverend Donald Harrington discussed these issues and recommended a solution in a sermon entitled "How the War on Poverty Became a War against the Poor":

> The system would be streamlined, and administered by the Internal Revenue Service. The change-over would, of course, have to be gradual. But such a re-organization and refinement of our social welfare set-up is not beyond the intelligence and ingenuity of American social science. ...[6]

Organized clients in the WROs played a major role in the public debate on establishing a guaranteed annual income (GAI). Within three years of beginning their activism (that is, by 1968), welfare rights members had adopted an agenda similar to those of social-work and welfare professionals, and forged a coalition among those same welfare officials who had come to symbolize the enemy. These unlikely allies — joined by other grass-roots reformists with similar interests — campaigned for acceptance of the GAI. New York City's welfare rights leaders — the late Beulah Sanders, Citywide[7] president; Hubert James, former director of Citywide; and Welfare Commissioner Mitchell Ginsberg; among others — testified at local and national budget hearings regarding the enactment of a federal guaranteed annual income. Proponents declared it to be a logical alternative to the increasing number of people on welfare.

Pressure from this welfare rights coalition escalated. WRO demonstrations — especially in the District of Columbia — may have prompted former President Richard Nixon to introduce to the public a Family Assistance Plan (FAP) in 1969. By doing so he acknowledged that the nation's welfare program and operational responsibility should be assumed by the federal government. *Time* magazine on February 8, 1971, buttressed Nixon's position by devoting a substantial segment of that issue to the problem, in a feature entitled the "Welfare Maze." The article's national statistics were as compelling as the data from New York City in 1965 and 1966 (see Chapter 2). For instance, from 1960 to 1970 the number of people receiving ADC more than tripled, from 3.0 million to 9.5 million. Welfare costs more than quadrupled from $1 billion to $4.8 billion, administrative costs included. Moreover, this situation occurred in the midst of a national economic upturn. With these and similar data accumulating all over the country, FAP's victory seemed inevitable.

Then a major problem surfaced, which split the coalition and halted lobbying for the GAI. Nixon proposed an income of $1,600 a year for a family of four. Welfare rights groups and many African-American leaders as well as social activists opposed the FAP, because the minimum income was too low. Another primary concern was the certain loss of at least $3,000 in benefits by current recipients in states like New York—although Mississippians, for instance, would gain by the plan because their current allotments were far lower. The U.S. Labor Department listed $5,500 as the minimum income that a family of four needed for survival.

Proponents of the plan maintained that even a $1,600 federal GAI was an improvement over the present economic status of poor people. Acknowledging that the proposed sum was small, advocates pointed out that an increase could be obtained once the GAI concept had become the law of the land. Welfare rights activists and supporters disagreed with that premise, noting that legislative amendments or policy changes would take months—even years. Furthermore, WRO members could not support any plan that would mean increased suffering among their own constituents or for their own immediate families. Consequently, FAP was defeated by a coalition of welfare rights members and middle-class activists. The scuttling of FAP sent GAI advocates back to the beginning—to rewrite the bill and identify sympathetic members of Congress who would be willing to sponsor it. In addition, they needed to reestablish the coalition lobby. As John Sullivan wrote in 1968:

and lurking in the background are those who, like Daniel Patrick Moynihan of the Harvard MIT Joint Center on Urban Affairs would like to see the United States adopt an integrated "family policy" whose conscious aim would be to improve the quality of family life in the nation. . . . The United States does have a family policy, notes Moynihan — and a pretty bad one — made up of income tax laws, aid to education, welfare and who knows what else. The question we face now is do we want to bring these together and consciously formulate a good family policy. . . . The United States is almost alone among the industrialized nations of the west in its haphazard approach to family life.[8]

True enough, but the process of formulating such a policy was likely to be lengthy — noted several of my respondents — perhaps as long as 20 years. In the interim, immediate needs had to be met with sufficient funds allocated for maintenance of decent living standards. Hubert James, former Citywide director, raised similar concerns in the same article:

How can you sit there and talk about something twenty years away, he shouted at Moynihan. . . . There are people starving, kids with rat bites and disease because this society won't help them. When are we going to wake up to that?

Currently — in 1988 — Moynihan is New York State's Democratic senator. He is the leading proponent of a welfare reform plan — the first major revision since 1935 — that passed the Senate in June 1988. It is slated for the Joint Congressional Committee as soon as possible. Although President Reagan has threatened a veto, congressional override is nearly a certainty because the legislation passed by significant margins in both houses of Congress. The plan includes putting ADC women to work outside the home. It is likely that many of them will join the ranks of the working poor. A GAI is not part of the plan. Obviously, the 20-year wait by James was a realistic time frame.[9]

VISTA WORKERS SERVING WITH A GRASS ROOTS MOVEMENT

The Volunteers in Service to America were crucial to the proliferation of WROs in central Brooklyn, and were an integral component of empowerment strategies. The activist priests of Bedford Stuyvesant applied for and obtained VISTA workers for welfare rights organizing. VISTA was a federal program administered by the Office of Economic Opportunity (OEO), essentially for the purpose of assisting people obtain a measure of grass roots power over the institutions in their communities. Securing the services of VISTA for welfare rights activities was an important achievement. With the VISTAs' participation, welfare rights organizing expanded dramatically. Overall responsibility for the VISTA workers rested with the churchmen, but welfare rights leaders provided daily supervision.

Never having been to New York City before, the new "VISTAs' experienced culture shock the first couple of weeks because they were sent almost immediately into the community, with less than a week of orientation."[10] Born and raised primarily in the West and Midwest, and having had virtually no personal contact with people of color, the volunteers were suddenly thrust into the everyday company of African-American and Hispanic people. Furthermore, women-of-color welfare recipients were their direct supervisors. In this environment, previous assumptions about economically disadvantaged people's anxieties and requisites quickly vanished. Instead the VISTAs acquired firsthand information on the hardships encountered by those on welfare:

> Often we witnessed situations that shocked us. We began to realize that people were virtually the same regardless of race or class, with similar aspirations and hopes for their families.[11]

Although VISTAs assisted in the formation and growth of the various welfare rights groups in Brooklyn, they had no decision-making roles. The recipients themselves decided how a new group would be administered. The VISTAs' daily responsibilities included visiting clients' homes (for recruitment purposes), assisting in the formation of committees, helping to represent clients at welfare centers, as well as identifying and developing potential leaders. Working in teams, the VISTA men and women functioned well, earning the welfare community's support and respect. Problems, hurts, and happiness were shared by clients, priests, and VISTAs. The degree of the community's general acceptance was evidenced by the fact that no VISTAs were harmed during the 1967 or 1968 rebellions, while they continued to live and organize in those same tense neighborhoods.

In most respects the VISTA presence was a positive experience for all parties, despite some problems. Brooklyn welfare rights leaders and VISTA officials from the national office in Washington, D.C., were uncomfortable with one another. The latter often objected to WRO activities as well as to the assignments given to VISTAs. There were instances of serious arguments and philosophical differences about the community institutions, between WROs and VISTA National. Brooklyn's VISTAs were loyal to WRO, regardless of any such disagreements. When their assignment ended, many continued to live in the community for months, and one stayed for six years. Volunteer Jim Baily may have been speaking for the majority of Brooklyn's VISTAs in the summer of 1968, when he said in an article:

If welfare mothers don't win their rights through peaceful pressure, their children, sensing their degradation and seeing the public discrimination against them, may join the growing revolution in the urban streets.

A guaranteed annual income is one means of eliminating discrimination and degradation around the country. It would help reunite many families. It would give welfare children new hope in their effort to break the poverty cycle. It would end abject poverty in the South.

We, the majority, must begin supporting all indigenous reform groups — for they are our hope for peaceful change — whether they are welfare groups, housing groups, or community job seekers and unions.[12]

The VISTAs discerned the weaknesses of the economic system and were frustrated by the absence of any substantive solutions to the problems confronting the lower strata of society. Their disappointment fostered a determination to organize people in order to pressure the government for more relevant programs.

In sum, organizing and demonstrations increased in Brooklyn, together with client self-confidence and respect. Said Ms. Samuels, "the ladder of success was within reach." With the arrival of the VISTAs, WRO activities assumed a new dimension, portending a time for major initiatives.

NOTES

1. Elizabeth Hood, "Black Women, White Women: Separate Paths to Liberation," *Black Scholar* 14 (September–October 1983): 26–37.

2. In the 1980s the poverty of households headed by white females has been documented, along with the plight of black females. Some people contend that the problem is now receiving a more thorough review, with calls for new ideas and programs to meet these families' needs. A fledgling body of literature has surfaced concerning the *feminization of poverty*. But simultaneously, the black family continues to be criticized, with black women and pregnant teens being blamed for problems that actually stem from the record unemployment levels in their communities. Their image has been tarnished: "From these unhealthy families and pathological communities flow the diseases of poverty, low educational achievement, prostitution, drug abuse and unemployment. This line of reasoning establishes the black woman as the evil one, rather than the victim." Hood, "Black Women, White Women."

3. One former client activist recalled during a summer 1983 interview in Brooklyn, New York, that she had joined the movement because of an encounter with welfare rights organizers on this issue.

4. New York *Reporter*, November 15, 1969. This weekly newspaper is no longer published.

5. *Flatbush Life*, February 22, 1969.

6. Sermon presented in 1982 at the Community Church of New York.

7. The Citywide Coordinating Council of Welfare Rights Groups (Citywide) — founded in 1965 and located in Manhattan — was the umbrella organization for all New York City boroughs, including B-WAC, established in November 1967.

8. John R. Sullivan, "Welfare System Saves Neither People Nor Money," *Tablet*, March 21, 1968.

9. In the Senate, the Family Welfare Reform Act of 1987 — known as #S1511 — is sponsored primarily by Daniel Patrick Moynihan, D-NY; in the House — where it is #HR1720 — Harold Ford, D-TN, is the lead person. *Congressional Quarterly Weekly Report* 46, #9–1988; and also *Congressional Record Index* 133 (1987). It passed in October 1988 as Public Law #100–145.

10. From the author's 1983 interview with a former VISTA worker, in Chicago.

11. Ibid.

12. James Baily, "Welfare Mothers Become Militant," *Tablet*, July 14, 1968.

5

The Brooklyn Welfare Action Council: Forty-Six Welfare Rights Member Groups

In 1967 the proliferation of storefront centers, the expansion of WRO membership throughout Brooklyn, and increased demonstrations and activities suggested the need for a coordinating body—that is, a unifying council or boroughwide executive committee. To that end, many community and borough meetings were held to determine how best to effectuate a federation. Welfare rights members decided to establish a coordinating council for Brooklyn. Information about preformation, purpose, and function were disseminated to all local welfare rights groups. Welfare rights leaders were asked to report members' comments to the ad hoc planning committee (for a coordinating council). Flyers were distributed throughout the neighborhoods listing the ad hoc members' names and the agenda for the first meeting. At that time a draft constitution was offered and accepted by the membership.

The developing concept and the actual council (the Brooklyn Welfare Action Council, or B-WAC) were funded by Catholic Charities of Brooklyn. Its initial budget was $5,000, not counting the one staff salary of $5,000. By 1971 the budget had risen to $12,000.[1] Total WRO grants disbursed by Catholic Charities between 1966 and 1973 was guesstimated at a half million dollars—with average storefront grants being about $8,500, according to church officials.

By the time the need for a council was recognized and acted on, 46 storefront centers representing almost every Brooklyn neighborhood had been established, mostly under the nuns' and priests' auspices. Similar groups formed as part of the federally sponsored Community Action Program (CAP) also joined the coordinating council. However, the welfare action centers organized by Fathers Matthews and Stevens were the strongest, and constituted nearly half the coalition. A measure of the action centers' strength and unity is that this group formed a separate entity and named it the Central Brooklyn Coordinating Group (CBCG). Their constitution and officers were almost identical with B-WAC's, since the member groups of CBCG included NAC, FAC, and other Brooklyn welfare rights organizations. Again Catholic Charities funded the group, and it too was operated by recipients. Near the end of the Brooklyn welfare rights movement—in 1971—the Brooklyn diocese assumed full administrative responsibilities for the member centers (as noted in Chapter 3). They became neighborhood service centers, staffed primarily by nonresident professionals.

The priests' role—although changed from the earliest storefront days—was vital in B-WAC's formation. They lobbied for the groups, introducing individual members and the welfare rights cause to influential people. Father Matthews and Father Stevens assumed the responsibilities of fundraising and scheduling speaking engagements for recipients, with the honorariums (usually paid by a middle-class organization) going to the council. Further, the priests convinced and arranged for church officials to meet with the welfare rights women regarding the proposed federation. Meeting with the bishop was yet another step in the empowerment of the recipients. Speaking to assemblies and lobbying those with authority increased the self-confidence and respect of welfare rights members. The clergymen's role was that of brokering and negotiating across racial, class, and gender barriers — a feat that would have been nearly insurmountable for the women alone. Their appreciation of these efforts enhanced the women's eloquence in presenting their own case once the doors had been opened to them.

But despite these noteworthy accomplishments of all involved, problems did surface. Some local groups — fearing a loss of autonomy — opposed the federation. Others worried about creating a bureaucracy that would mirror the institutions they were pledged to change. And — according to several respondents — the Citywide Coordinating Council of Welfare Rights Groups (with headquarters in Manhattan) and the National Welfare Rights Organization (based in the District of Columbia) had qualms about the potential strength of the Brooklyn group. They knew that it could become the largest local welfare rights entity in the country. Its capacity to supersede Citywide and possibly NWRO — or simply to cease its affiliation with them — caused much concern.

None of those issues were real, because B-WAC's president, Joyce Burson, had strong loyalties to both Citywide and NWRO. She knew the importance of unity, and promoted that notion at every level — at meetings, in discussions, and with individual members. Citywide's and NWRO's fears were groundless. Nevertheless, the two organizations remained suspicious of Brooklyn's motives.

Citywide's director between 1967 and 1969 — Hulbert James — acknowledged the Brooklyn priests' expertise and dedication to recipient empowerment, agreeing that their efforts had resulted in the development of a cadre of indigenous leaders. In other cities — James noted that white male organizers dominated decision-making, but not so in Brooklyn. B-WAC participants always knew precisely why a specific demonstration or action was necessary. James believed the reason for this was that

> members discussed and voted on all activities, in addition
> to planning and organizing the events. If B-WAC par-
> ticipants decided against an action then it was abandoned,
> regardless of the priests' position on the issue.[2]

Brooklyn had hundreds of organized clients who were loyal
to B-WAC. Demonstrations not approved by the organization
received almost no support in the borough. A large active
membership—completely loyal and disciplined—was B-
WAC's primary strength. There was another equally important
factor in its success: leadership training for and by people
receiving public assistance.

B-WAC: A CONSTITUTION AND NEW HEADQUARTERS

B-WAC became an official entity in November 1967. Initially
housed in the downtown Brooklyn offices of Catholic Charities'
social action department, it was soon relocated to Bushwick
Avenue. This site was a large, uninhabited (except for a caretaker
and his family), three-story, detached Victorian house, which had
formerly been a German social club; it was a legacy from Father
Matthews, who had obtained it rent free for welfare rights purposes. The owners were glad that it was being used, since the threat
of vandalism would then ease. Welfare rights members appreciated their new headquarters, for it was convenient and comfortable. Meetings and classes held there were well attended.

Meanwhile, the work of establishing the federation and
finalizing the constitution proceeded at a fast pace, due to the
dedication and efforts of B-WAC's first staff person, Rhoda
Linton.[3] Completed and approved by the members in 1967, the
council's constitution stated:

> The Brooklyn Welfare Action Council will be composed
> of Welfare Rights Organizations in the Borough of Brook-

lyn. The primary aim of the Council will be to work on problems of Welfare Recipients directly related to the Department of Social Services [Welfare]. For example, the Council will coordinate joint group actions and organize leadership training programs for the benefit of all groups. Other problems not directly related to the Department of Social Services, such as setting up co-op housing, action on school issues, etc., may be dealt with as long as they do not interfere with the primary purpose.[4]

B-WAC's constitution became a model for all Brooklyn groups. In some cases local WRO constitutions were changed to complement it. The former president of NAC was elected B-WAC's first president. With Catholic Charities funding, B-WAC hired two staff members — a black woman[5] and a Jewish male VISTA worker — as coordinator and office manager, respectively.

LEADERSHIP AND MEMBER TRAINING

B-WAC's strong recruitment strategy and leadership training were the keys to its success. Because its training was offered in a nurturing and sharing atmosphere, people with limited formal education attended the classes without fear of embarrassment. The curriculum and materials received special attention regarding clarity, brevity, and appropriateness for different reading levels.

Two dedicated white middle-class supporters of welfare rights, who had been longtime community activists,[6] accepted the difficult assignment of developing a curriculum that would address the varying educational levels of students and trainers who had been away from the classroom for a long time, while also acknowledging that the students had a reservoir of practical life-experience. Using those characteristics as guidelines and with substantial assistance from the clients, they drafted a curriculum that focused on low-income adult needs. It acknowledged and built on student and trainer backgrounds in the context of the African-American and Hispanic experiences. Flexibility was incorporated into the training materials, thus providing an opportunity for the indigenous trainers to personalize and shape each course or session. A tribute to the efforts of the curriculum's developers was evidenced by the respect, enthusiasm, and overflow crowds at each session, which included nonmembers, people from out of town, and even some local officials.

Instituted in January 1968, the leadership development curriculum offered five separate areas of study, of which three classes (A, B, and C) proved very popular. At one point, requests for the first two increased to such a degree that the classes were held every week for two months. Members registered for the classes through their local group or at the B-WAC office itself, where the classes were held in various rooms. Fostering empowerment, developing political awareness, and helping people to help themselves were the program's long-range goals. The classes' specific objectives[7] were:

Class A   to provide opportunity for every individual B-WAC member to learn her right to services under the present law, and how to get them; and to discuss possible changes in the system.

Class B   to provide opportunity for every B-WAC group to learn how to organize a welfare rights organization (leaders, volunteers, advisors, and elected or appointed representatives of groups could attend so long as they were approved by the local group as that group's representatives).

Class C   to provide opportunity for every B-WAC group (through group representatives) to learn how to plan and carry out actions — that is, picketing, demonstrations and sit-ins.

Two other classes' goals were:

> *Class D*   to provide opportunity for all members of the council to discuss the background and the future of the welfare rights movement.
>
> *Class E*   to provide opportunity for every B-WAC group—according to section or area of the borough (through group representatives)—to learn about its own community: Who makes decisions (identifying the politicians, the business people, and the heads of institutions)? Who are the elected politicians? What really makes the community tick?

Many subjects listed in the curriculum for Classes D and E were also discussed in A, B, or C. Flexibility and informality allowed for subject interchanging, additions, and deletions. But actually Class D, which was to discuss the future of the movement, was never offered separately. We shall see that this was a serious error in judgment.

During periods when classes were in progress, the activity inside B-WAC's building resembled total chaos. The roles of teachers and students were changing constantly. Morning teachers of Class A became afternoon students in Class C. Visitors—usually social workers—were numerous; they listened, questioned, and sometimes participated in the sessions. Visitors were amazed by the recipients' acuity, and by the fact that clients were teaching other clients. Local college students requested and received unsalaried internships at B-WAC; these included majors in law, sociology, and social work. Human service organizations sent their staff as observers to the classes and public meetings, in an attempt to sensitize employees about problems that clients faced. In addition, these agency staff were receiving firsthand knowledge that illustrated the recipients' self-growth potential. In many instances, interaction between the visitors and B-WAC members fostered a climate of mutual respect and friendship.

Observers were welcome, and even frequently invited. But as classrooms started to approach the saturation point, the visiting trainees and observers were a cause of disruption to the classes; hence the number of guests was drastically reduced. Members discussed this step before taking it, and numerous questions arose: Were B-WAC's resources adequate for training nonmembers? Could or should B-WAC charge visitors and observers a service fee? Was B-WAC evolving into a service and training institution for middle-class professionals, and was this a desirable state of affairs? What impact would this situation have on current and future B-WAC members? With the increased numbers of visitors, clients were becoming reluctant to attend, because—as the interviewees said—"clients were ashamed and nervous about being in class with professionals." Principals felt that there existed the possibility of actual usurpation of B-WAC's vision of recipient control and service. Thus, out of a fear that B-WAC's constitutional mandate might come to be circumscribed, guests were virtually barred. The space left by the visitors was quickly filled by clients.

MOBILIZING ORGANIZED RECIPIENTS

As a result of these classes, Brooklyn's organized recipients were—in many areas of welfare law and policy—the most knowledgeable and well trained in the country, according to activists and organizers in other groups. B-WAC students committed to memory all New York State's welfare laws and established policies, along with the ones that were periodically revised. Privately, caseworkers admitted that the welfare rights' members had more information about the department's structure than did staff. The recipients knew how to use that structure to obtain maximum benefits or concessions for B-WAC members. Ms. Wise remembers that

> B-WAC had people in the welfare center every day organizing, advocating for and representing clients. Brook-

lyn groups covered all the borough's fourteen welfare centers. Their responsibilities were enormous, for example, at case conferences, a family's or client's problems were discussed; a WRO member attended the meeting and advised clients of their rights. Fair hearings, little known and seldom used prior to welfare rights organizing, was an appeal process for clients denied funds or services. Members accompanied clients to the hearing and functioned in a manner similar to a paralegal attorney. Under WR's guidance this process was used extensively to secure benefits illegally withheld by local social service centers. Also, B-WAC and other WROs obtained critical concessions regarding fair hearings, i.e., shorter delays for a hearing date or an answer, the assigning of additional hearing staff, hearings sometimes held in the community at reasonable hours, hearings held in the home or hospital, if necessary. Any [individual] member group having problems in a center would call B-WAC and all groups demonstrated at the unyielding center.[8]

Therein lay B-WAC's primary strength: the ability to mobilize hundreds of clients. So overwhelming was the response to such a muster, that staff and officers became increasingly selective about the number of groups that they would contact. Members believed that an exaggerated response to a problem could diminish B-WAC's effectiveness with department officials and with its own membership.

Despite its early successes, B-WAC actually had no long-term goals. This shortsightedness was a critical weakness. Issues regarding the future should have been discussed in Class D, but it was never held. The formal establishment of a training institution might have been one outcome.

Brooklyn was strong enough to have been very influential in the political process. B-WAC did not go through to the next step (the political arena). We were politically naive. Father Stevens admits he didn't move us to the next level.

Real politics were threatening to us — we stayed away from politicians. Lindsay was clobbered for being too lenient with us. Either B-WAC's or Lindsay's staff should have seen this as a way or reason to bring us into the political arena. B-WAC could have been a very effective force in Lindsay's campaign for re-election.[9]

Leader after former leader discussed the lack of long-term goals or plans for the "next step." Bitter and sad reactions concerning this organizational defect were more common than diplomatic comments such as these of Ms. Dorchester:

It [welfare rights organizing] gave people self-confidence and self-respect, [but we] needed other goals. . . . The *next steps* would have been found provided that the core people or head [president] had not left. Staff should have provided new questions or goals. But I'm not sure that the staff was paid to take us another step, they may [or may not] have known other steps but only did their job [what they were hired to do — administration]. Even the support groups or NWRO did not assist us in going to the next level.[10]

QUESTIONS AND STRATEGIES THAT DIVIDED WRO MEMBERS AND STAFF

In retrospect during the interviews, former members were puzzled by the lack of future goals; they questioned the B-WAC staff's commitment to substantive change, implying that cultural barriers had mitigated against their taking a new direction. Did the staff's class biases concerning poor people's ability to absorb and execute abstract issues prevent them from recommending that B-WAC accept fresh political initiatives? Or was the staff so limited that other approaches simply never surfaced in their consciousness? On the other hand, were they concerned that the recipients would depart from establishment concepts and proceed to embrace a radical vision of social change that could threaten the staff's own middle-class values? If that were the case, they need not have worried. B-WAC members had middle-class aspirations, which became ever more apparent as they obtained a degree of upward mobility. Hence, their traditional views regarding women and family changed only slightly. Perhaps, beneath the surface, the staff members were indeed more conservative than members perceived, or less certain of clients' potential than they cared to admit. Still, some questions remain: Why did members wait for instructions or a new direction? Had not the time arrived for them to assume the responsibility of articulating their own goals to the staff? Did the departure of the B-WAC president[11] extinguish any embryonic attempts at developing untried methods or programs that would advance social equity? And, in general, what are activists' prospects after their movement ends and the opposition escalates its efforts against the participants? These questions have not been approached in this present study, but they do warrant further research. Perhaps the initially traditional nature of B-WAC lessened its chances of entering into dialogue with staff and participants regarding new directions.

Moreover, its service image may have contributed to the dilemma. Fainstein and Fainstein have observed that

> groups we studied relied on three major mobilization strategies: (1) utopian appeals, (2) professional organizers, (3) service provisions. The service approach . . . while successful in attracting poor people to community organizations has failed to create organizations with a political purpose.[12]

These two authors provide no definitive answer as to why these organizations failed to adopt a political agenda. However, B-WAC's experience does support their view.

Gender considerations may have caused the B-WAC staff's reluctance to foster more radical responses. Yet one could maintain that the members were less independent of the staff than the staff may even have believed, and more afraid of taking a radical course. Regarding the composition of community organizations, Fainstein and Fainstein continue:

> In each of our lengthy case studies women were predominant among movement leadership though not always in the top position; [this is true] especially in groups which are predominately black.[13]

This observation supports other studies suggesting that women as direct users of community institutions and agencies are more involved with improving them than men.[14] Out of necessity, women respond to the experience of daily or routine inequities by uniting and promoting change for their families and themselves. In the 1960s, community organizing was still the domain of women, while the activism of men was considered to be national and worldwide in scope.

B-WAC's predicament as an institution without a future was an important statement about organizational control by poor women of color—one that social planners and organizers would do well to heed. At a given juncture in a movement's life span, the participants' class and gender interests will manifest themselves and come into conflict. Activists from a wealthier class have to make some fundamental a priori decisions regarding their involvement in the poor people's movement: whether—as an organization matures—they will leave, or remain and lower their profile; and whether they will support or stifle radical thoughts. Organizers may suddenly discover that the people they organized now consider them part of the problem. If these circumstances occur the organizers should be proud, for this signals that they have done their job well and that the time to leave is past due.

Cloward and Piven argue in *Poor People's Movements : Why They Succeed, How They Fail* that B-WAC reached or passed its utility when it left the streets and abandoned disruptive tactics. The authors posit that there was a direct correlation between B-WAC's waning power and its emphasis on being a dues-paying service organization that was moving toward institutionalization: "We maintain that political influence by the poor is mobilized, not organized."[15]

The verdict is still out on the issue of mobilization versus organization. In defense of the latter, activists maintain that disenfranchised people should secure knowledge about the political process and its impact on their social as well as economic circumstances. It is politically and morally imperative that they know why they must demonstrate. Lack of political awareness leaves poor people unprotected against demagogues. Consequently, they run the risk of having their bodies used in the street actions without their informed consent.

RENEWED CONSERVATISM IN NEW YORK CITY

Welfare clients faced renewed hardships in the summer of 1968, largely because there was a backlash building against them. Many middle-class families — black and white — were disillusioned about high taxes and expenditures for programs that had failed to attain their stated goals, as noted by the first HRA commissioner, Mitchell Svirdoff.[16] The city's political environment responded to the changing attitudes of its constituents. Mayor Lindsay was reticent about the brutality of the New York police against welfare rights demonstrators who were mainly women and children — and yet he was critical of Chicago police tactics. On Thursday, August 29, 1968, the New York *Post* carried an article called "Lindsay Scores Chi Police" that reported Lindsay's criticism of the police action at the Democratic National Convention in Chicago:

"What happened last night in Chicago should sadden every American," he said. "I hope what happened there will stand as a warning to those who have perverted the meaning of 'law and order' and made it the sole answer to our nation's problems.... For last night in Chicago, there was neither law nor order, nor justice." As he read a prepared statement . . . nearly 100 police—foot and mounted, uniform and plainclothes, massed in the City Hall area in anticipation of a third day of welfare demonstrations.

In the editorial section of the same edition, the *Post* noted that

> The Lindsay administration in contrast has taken the dramatically opposite approach [from Chicago] despite such lamentable incidents as the unduly harsh crackdown on welfare demonstrators at City Hall this week.

The reference here was to the four days (August 27 through 30, 1968) of City Hall demonstrations by WRO groups against the city's having established a flat grant, which replaced the separate minimum-standard checks. From that time on, clients would receive $100 a year for all special items other than the basics of rent and food.

Protesting against this new system, welfare rights members had to contend with mounted police. According to the New York *Post* on August 27, 1968 ("Cops, Welfare Clients Clash; 12 Held"), top Lindsay aides—including Sid Davidoff and Barry Gotteher—watched as foot police used nightsticks on women while mounted police rode into picket lines, injuring women and children. In the New York *Times* on August 28, 1968, Carl Rachlin—a welfare rights lawyer—declared that "there was no excuse for horses." His comment was well taken, since the mounted police had a reputation—among activists—for being abusive in demonstrations. News accounts listed nine injured and 36 arrested, while WRO members said that the numbers were at least double that. "Screaming women," according to the *Times*, "charged that the police wouldn't do this to white people."

With a more conservative federal administration and the mounting popular backlash against recipient demands throughout the city, organized clients discovered that an increase in the number of arrests was forecasting a shift to a less sympathetic stance by the city administration, as well. Communication between participants and officials lessened considerably. This retrenchment by authorities prompted attempts by WRO activists to move toward compromise and conciliation and to abandon confrontation amid efforts to protect recent gains. The circumstances were an inevitable dysfunction of the movement. WRO participants and organizers were unprepared for the reversal and accompanying crackdown. Although the movement's theorists were aware of this possibility, they had underestimated how swiftly action would be taken.

Of necessity, WRO's (citywide) efforts assumed a different character: It left the streets and took to the meeting rooms. But WRO and city officials were now far apart, with the former ready to negotiate or compromise while the power holders remained unyielding. This departure from protests to meeting-room negotiations damaged the movement's credibility with its members.[17] According to numerous rumors, Citywide leaders were "selling out" the movement.

By the 1970s self-confidence among organized clients had waned because the expected gains that should have accrued from lobbying and negotiating never materialized. These setbacks provided new evidence to support Cloward and Pivens in their mobilization versus organization theory. Advocates learned a lesson: that negotiation and compromise must be conducted between equals. WRO's constituents had little power, and few connections with influential people and institutions. Their disadvantages were evident, and their few highly placed administration friends had grown weary of the struggle. Remaining allies supported the WRO's abandonment of disruptive strategies,[18] but were too few to influence officials and professionals. At this juncture, a description of the specific activities that prompted this state of affairs would be useful.

MAJOR DEMONSTRATIONS LED BY B-WAC

When welfare rights members initially assembled at the welfare centers, they were determined to change the nature of the system by pressing for funds that were being illegally withheld. As one former leader observed, they had been caught in a maze without an exit. Everyone related to the system was its victim, including both department personnel and clients. As they used the system, so the system used them—needing and obtaining the cooperation of all the players in order to endure. This systemic schizophrenia was reflected in the welfare rights members and their movement.

William Gamson has said:

> For men to plunge headlong into an undertaking of vast change they must be intensely discontented yet not destitute—they must have an extravagant concept for the future: they must be ignorant of the difficulties involved—experience is a handicap. [Conversely] conventional groups act to achieve goals rather than reacting to express distress.[19]

In relating that passage to WRO, one discerns that the women were indeed seeking to achieve major goals at the peak of welfare rights organizing.[20] At the same time, there was little doubt about welfare rights participants' innocence and inexperience regarding the difficulties that awaited them. Yet the members persevered and organized a movement with strategies that were creative and unconventional, as a description of their demonstrations will illustrate.

Minimum Standards Campaign

The first action of the NAC activists—securing minimum standards grants—had been principally self-serving.[21] However, these future B-WAC members received an important lesson in unity, since all participants stayed until everyone's checks were distributed. Some might argue that the experience was more a lesson in socialism than unity, and that welfare rights' glorification of a group effort by low- and grant-income people had revolutionary overtones. This argument has no relevance in the case of B-WAC members, because they were patriotic, loyal to capitalism, and scornful of anyone discussing a different system of government. B-WAC participants knew this country's weaknesses—to be sure—but they were confident that it provided enough range for them to promote economic and social changes. Perhaps—as we shall see—they were too confident.

New members were grateful for the help in securing minimum standards grants and were curious about the organization. Hence they returned to the local welfare rights centers and volunteered their time. Minimum standards drives were so numerous that they became routine, institutionalized organizing exercises for new members and training grounds for novice client representatives. It was not uncommon for a welfare recipient who had been fearful of the department's response to her application—but at the same time hopeful that the promise of special funds by welfare rights organizers would not prove false—to find herself 1–10 days later representing clients with problems identical to her own. She was speaking out— challenging officials, and demanding equity and dignity. As the organized recipients' confidence grew emotionally, they progressed light-years in little more than a week. Ms. Halstrum, a respondent, described the situation thus:

> We were used to begging. We never demanded anything— welfare rights enabled us to walk in a welfare center unafraid, dignified and secure in the knowledge that our needs would be met.
> And they were.

Special-Needs Demonstrations

After participating in minimum standards demonstrations, NAC (and later, all B-WAC) found other department actions to be less difficult. Brooklyn members campaigned and obtained funds for laundry, graduation, confirmation, camp, gym, and spring clothes as well as layettes and washing machines. Because members had been unaware that they could request this assistance, they greatly appreciated the grants for these items. Special-needs money offered their children new opportunities. The children could now participate in gym classes, attend camp with the required clothing, be confirmed, or take part in graduation ceremonies. Also, successful welfare rights actions generated enough funds to remove the need for making a choice between buying food and washing one's clothes.

Several former recipients recalled their efforts to receive a special-needs check, the frustrations that they experienced, and the suffering that their children had endured from lack of money for school clothes and other items. On July 16, 1968, in the *Tablet*, a caseworker depicted one welfare center's response to the clothing grant drive:

> For many of them their day began at 6 a.m. when they walked to the blond-brick building at 485 State St. The Welfare people had told them to come to get lighter clothing for their children. . . . So they came, gave their names and addresses and were told to have a seat and they would soon be taken care of. . . . A mother, worn-out by the daylong wait, [was] sobbing plaintively to an equally weary center-worker. "Please help me, I've been here since 6 this morning and my poor children don't have any clothes. Please help me.". . . Perhaps the most significant voice heard was that of another caseworker: "This might be a good thing that's happening. Maybe somebody will realize that you can't use 1930 methods to deal with welfare cases in the 1960's."[22]

Admittedly the crowded conditions were partly the result of welfare rights organizing. Nonmembers learned about clothing drives and visited the Welfare Department to request grants. Many acted independently of welfare rights groups. Members and nonmembers alike waited for service, while clients continued arriving with other problems: evictions, fires, or burglaries, for example. WRO's disruptive strategies against the bureaucracy succeeded, but the price was psychologically prohibitive for both clients and the department staff. While WRO members were being served, problems requiring emergency attention would often be delayed. At times, the resentment from nonmembers was substantial.

These campaigns—which were, in actuality, recruiting tactics—encouraged many people to believe that the Welfare Department would soon be bankrupt. In response, the state legislature came to the system's rescue by enacting the flat grant in 1969. The basic needs of recipients were to be covered by this grant, excluding shelter, fuel, utilities, and items of special need. But two years prior to that legislation—in 1967—Nicholas Kisburg, research director for the International Brotherhood of Teamsters legislative department, had become increasingly concerned about welfare payments versus salaries. He issued a 12-page press release, citing persuasive data about the problem: During the first half of 1967, New York City (which was nearing the 1 million mark on public assistance, out of its 7 million people) had 660,634 ADC recipients—22 percent more than the same period in 1966. For clothing and furniture, in the first six months of 1965, clients had received a per capita yearly amount of $11.45. During the same period a year later, the per capita expenditure for the same purpose increased to $26.80 a year. These statistics made a convincing case for establishing a statutory minimum wage because, continued Kisburg, in the 1967 press release:

> abysmal as the allowances are, the welfare family of four has a larger take-home income than the same family head can net on the New York statutory wage of $1.50 per hour.

In truth, the situation warranted federalizing the welfare system. Similar publications advanced national debates concerning the feasibility of a guaranteed annual income. The

issue reached Congress, but—as explained previously—the
measure was defeated.

Telephone Service for All Recipients

Noting that the average American had telephone service by
the late 1960s, B-WAC members demanded the service mainly
because "poor people living in areas with greater health, housing and fire hazards and high crime rates had a more pressing
need; for most recipients it was literally a life line.[23] The
caseworkers' union—SSEU—supported the telephone campaign, saying,

> We feel that it is obviously an absolute necessity for
> everyone to have a phone. It should be put directly into
> the budget with other necessities.[24]

Even before the WRO campaign, the Welfare Department
could assume the monthly telephone costs of recipients provided
that it had written requests from a physician, hospital, or clinic; or
if the client could prove that the telephone would be useful in
obtaining employment, training, or business.[25] Most clients knew
nothing about this policy and thus did not apply. Hulbert James
observed that, in high crime areas, finding an operating—public
or private—telephone late at night because of a sick child or other
emergency was dangerous on at least two counts: First, it could
mean leaving a child alone; and second, the parent—usually a
woman—had to search the community by herself.

The telephone was a communication line as well as a symbol
of connection to the ladder of success. At this campaign's end,
many clients still had no phones, but most handicapped or
special-cases clients who applied did receive more sympathetic
responses from department staff. Many recipients lost the
feeling that having a telephone was a luxury, after it became a
public issue. In essence, the public began to understand the
necessity of a telephone—especially for slum residents—yet
continued to oppose the campaign because of the program's

potential costs. The Welfare Department supported that position. Robert Carroll stated, "Under present operating policy of the city, telephone service paid by the department will not be authorized for any reason other than medical."[26] Regardless of the department's stand, this campaign succeeded in advancing first-time demands for items that were beyond life's basic necessities. Clients had given notice that they were striving for the tools to improve their living conditions. The telephone was just one of these required items. Other quality-of-life targets were coming into focus.

B-WAC's underlying agenda included helping people to leave the public assistance rolls and enter the mainstream. Members knew that social supports — like the B-WAC organization — played an important role in this effort. Participants no longer in need of welfare were models for other clients: There was a celebration every time someone secured a full-time job. Concomitantly, organized clients realized that most recipients had no alternative to welfare and would remain dependent on the system. Thus, organizers set about developing positive concepts and options for the majority of B-WAC members. Acquiring credentials and skills training was strongly encouraged. At the same time, the organizers helped clients to face reality about the unlikelihood of obtaining employment that would offer a salary adequate enough to make them self-sufficient and free of the welfare system. Accordingly, B-WAC promoted discussions concerning social or political unsalaried community participation that was as important as salaried work. In essence, people could make contributions to improving the quality of community life regardless of their employment status. Former members agreed that organizers were relatively successful in this effort and that most members were pledged to a continuing civic involvement. One activist observed that, although a higher place on the economic and social ladder might elude them, for their sons and daughters it was within reach — provided the parents continue as social change advocates.

The Struggle for an Equitable Utilities Policy

The telephone service battle raised larger issues concerning utilities in general. For years, recipients had complained about the electric and gas companies' insensitivity. Their swift disconnection policy often resulted in the creation of life-threatening situations for the very young and old—particularly when it came to a lack of heat, loss of the means to cook, or no lights to ward off rats. The members' response included mounting actions against shutoffs at the gas and electric offices. Every former member told me that observing the dignity and aggressiveness of WRO participants had prompted their joining these utility campaigns as well as the organization itself. Organized recipients pressed for the cessation of shutoffs during winter months, and in-person shutoff warnings (because of unreliable mail service, many notices never arrived) as well as authorizing utility representatives to accept partial payments. These were among the features that advocates urged for inclusion in a citywide utility policy. Last, B-WAC members demonstrated and pressed for the elimination of security deposits, since the clients' monthly allotment did not contain this item. (Deposits could vary from nothing to $500, depending on the neighborhood.) These demands were later adopted by the state and national welfare rights organizations.

Welfare Department officials agreed with the clients' stance, and joined the effort. They were often present, lending support at meetings that B-WAC or Citywide arranged with utility representatives.[27] Again, raising issues for public debate was the chief gain here; and educating the companies about recipients' inherent problems must also be counted as a victory. Respondents in my study believed that the welfare rights efforts resulted in uniform utility deposits (and in some cases, their elimination entirely), heat allowances being available to more people, and a decreasing number of winter shutoffs. In special cases concerning the elderly and handicapped, the Welfare Department would be contacted by the utility company regarding the delay of payments. Further, the welfare offices' implementation of procedures for expeditiously issuing utility (or rent) checks had its roots in B-WAC's efforts and other welfare rights organizing—as did the larger issue of degree of corporate responsibility to the community.

The Credit Campaign and Strategy

B-WAC's last major successful campaign—with the exception of the ongoing minimum standards drive—was the demonstration for an extension of financial credit to people receiving public assistance.[28] A carefully planned and implemented action, it highlighted the potential talents of unskilled people. The membership voted to challenge general credit policies and specifically those of Korvettes, a department store that was frequented by people on welfare. Before the campaign was consummated, B-WAC's officers were given the responsibility for negotiating a presettlement: That is, they offered the retailer an opportunity to extend credit prior to the onset of demonstrations. Korvettes officials either ignored B-WAC's warnings or miscalculated its strength. Consequently, on November 21, 1968, demonstrations were staged in and outside Korvettes in Brooklyn's major shopping area; they lasted five days.

At the end of that time, organized clients obtained between $25 and $100 of personal credit per client. As the NWRO national newsletter *NOW* said in December 1968:

New York groups have been conducting a campaign to get credit for welfare recipients from E. J. Korvettes stores. The campaign began in Brooklyn on November 21, 1968. . . . Negotiations are continuing with client groups demanding to be recognized as official representatives of welfare recipients.

Abraham & Strauss—a department store across the street from Korvettes that offered higher priced merchandise— voluntarily opened credit negotiations with B-WAC in the aftermath of the Korvettes demonstrations. By December, both stores had developed and instituted procedures to review credit applications submitted by people on welfare. Shortly after that, all grant-income recipients (including those on pensions, social security, and disability) were encouraged to apply for credit. In this struggle for equal financial access, minorities and all women were beneficiaries of the welfare recipients' actions. How they accomplished this feat was pure theater.

Background and Role Playing

People on welfare frequently complained about the fact that the only credit available to them was from loan sharks or small neighborhood businesses charging usurious interest rates. That fact set in motion the credit drive in Brooklyn and later across the country. The B-WAC staff was instructed to compile as much information as possible on Korvettes. Along with other data, they discovered the identity of the chain store's owners. Members of the Friends of Welfare Rights Organization (FWROs)[29] were asked to contact these individuals on the golf courses, at their private clubs, and—if necessary—at their places of worship for their support in providing credit to poor people with fixed income.

Moreover, FWROs agreed to raise the credit issue at a subsequent stockholders' meeting. Meanwhile, B-WAC members received special training in sessions that were essentially dress rehearsals for the action. After their completion, members were assigned to roles and responsibilities: *outside the store*—pickets, messengers, marshals, leafleters, and spokespersons (several for pedestrians, and one for the media); *inside the store*—fake customers (further divided between irate and sympathetic), real customers, and watchers or crowds (militants and moderates), plus representatives for negotiating with Korvettes' officials.

On the day of the demonstration, members impersonating customers selected hundreds of dollars worth of goods and took them to the cashiers, who proceeded to tally the items on their registers. When asked for payment, each "customer"30 produced her welfare identification card and said, "Charge it to the Welfare Department." Naturally, the cashier refused the card and then had to obtain assistance on clearing the register of the mock charge. This situation resulted in long lines at the cash registers; the same action was taking place simultaneously throughout the store. "Irate customers" standing in line with numerous expensive items — ostensibly to purchase them — voiced their displeasure about the delay, threatening to take their business elsewhere. Other clients grumbled to the un-suspecting real customers about the store's incompetence. "Crowds" formed quickly around the cash registers, aug-mented by the genuinely curious.

All this commotion at rush hour proved too much for Kor-vettes personnel. Clerks and managers tried to be reasonable, requesting that members discuss the issue with them in a quiet office. Clients refused to acquiesce. Finally, the store manager — later joined by Korvettes' regional representative — invited the demonstration leaders to negotiate. Despite objec-tions from some principals, the leaders agreed to Korvettes' proposal; but by then, law enforcement had been summoned. When word reached the inside demonstrators that police had arrived, participants left the area to forestall any threat of arrest. At the general membership meeting prior to the action, B-WAC members had voted against anyone being arrested.

By the time police reached the demonstration floors, every-thing had returned to normal except for piles of unbought clothing surrounding most of the cash registers. "Customers" were browsing alongside actual purchasers, waiting for the police to leave and the signal to begin the demonstration anew. When employees relaxed, a "customer" offered her welfare card in lieu of cash, and the whole process commenced again.

When things finally quieted down and negotiations began in earnest, the "moderates" agreed to discontinue the inside demonstrations until higher placed officials could be con-tacted. Late that evening, when welfare rights members left

Korvettes, they vowed to return the next day. This time, the management did not doubt their word.

Results of the Action

The demonstrators then met at a prearranged site – a nearby coffee shop – and evaluated the action. Chaired by the B-WAC coordinator, the session (along with the action) was a key politicizing and organizing tool. Members acquired as much knowledge at evaluation sessions as they did at demonstrations and leadership training classes. The sessions provided an opportunity for members to examine and weigh the merits of any action that they had planned. Demonstrators discussed the strengths and weaknesses of specific activities and individuals until after midnight, when finally they would head home from the day's action.

These meetings had another purpose: Staff and demonstrators wanted to prepare themselves for questions that the other members might raise. This was the only time that the participants in the credit action would meet before the full B-WAC membership received official news of the outcome. According to tradition, a borough meeting would be held no more than two days after any major action, to keep members informed of the results. These assemblies, after demonstrations, were well attended. Officers would describe the action and explain what was accomplished or lost; which goals were met, unmet, or changed, and why; and who failed or who was exemplary. This post credit action meeting was usually charged with emotion, but constructive criticisms were offered and accepted. As with most B-WAC gatherings, it was a training session, and everyone profited from the exercise.

Brooklyn's credit action, which was watched closely by clients around the country, precipitated nationwide welfare rights actions. The January 6, 1969, issue of *KNIC-NAC*, the welfare rights newsletter, reported that

The Brooklyn demonstration has snowballed into a national action. "Citywide" . . . has been negotiating with

Gimbels and other retail stores for credit, while national welfare rights has been contacted by Montgomery Ward and other stores eager to make an arrangement to extend credit nationwide. . . .

In the meantime, B-WAC has been contacted by Abraham & Strauss as to how they can work with the client groups rather than have demonstrations staged at their store. Korvetts [*sic*] so far has been the only store treated to the client action. However, all stores are more than a little uneasy due to the potential strength of the client groups.

The drive spanned several months. The New York *Times* became interested in the story after national actions were mounted against Sears, Roebuck and Co. stores. On July 20, 1969, the *Times* reported:

A disclosure [was made] that three of the city's department stores [Gimbels, Abraham & Strauss, and Korvettes] had individually agreed to extend credit to welfare recipients on the urging of the local unit of the national welfare rights organizations [NWRO].

B-WAC members negotiated with high-level officials in Brooklyn's retail industry and developed credit guidelines for people on fixed incomes. The primary topic of contention was Korvettes' insistence that B-WAC assume responsibility for the screening of potential credit holders and—as an organization—be responsible for untrustworthy clients. Specifically, clients eligible for credit had to be B-WAC members and previously investigated by the organization. A B-WAC membership card and letter would assure applicants that credit would be extended. But the organization's leaders were opposed to being credit examiners; they feared increased dissension among members, together with the potential for credit-related corruption. The members, however, voted in favor of the project because they believed that the credit line's importance outweighed Korvettes' stipulations.

A different type of member joined as a consequence of B-WAC's new role. The objective of these members concerned obtaining credit. They had little interest in welfare rights. These women did not volunteer time or attend meetings or training classes, despite repeated letters and visits by B-WAC representatives. After a few weeks — when B-WAC officers and staff had perfected the procedures of the project — they issued strict credit guidelines that required three months' *active* membership, references (other members' recommendations were preferable), and verification of a recipient's status and residence. Participants did not forget the initial confusion following their precedent-setting credit achievement. They realized that careful planning for the eventuality of success of an action was just as vital as preparations for its implementation.

Community Control: Schools, Welfare Centers

B-WAC participated in the 1968–69 demonstrations for community control of schools. Members viewed the schools as the chief institution fostering their own and their children's aspirations for upward mobility. Once community leaders exposed this institution's weaknesses and inequities, organized clients joined the effort to eliminate control of the schools by bureaucrats and people residing outside the community. The action was ongoing and supported by much of the community.[31] In a show of solidarity with Oceanhill-Brownsville's residents and elected officials, organized clients walked picket lines in support of community control, volunteered their services inside the schools, and encouraged their children to attend the schools that were on strike. Despite the energy and efforts of many people, the campaign there failed: It lacked substantial white support throughout the city.

The black educator Al Vann[32] was a leading critic of this country's and the city's education system. The New York

Amsterdam News on September 1, 1973, reported Vann as stating, in part,

> By and large black school children are not learning to read, are not learning arithmetic, are not learning to write. . . . Teachers are a very essential part of the educational structure and the educational process. Whatever is happening to our children, teachers deserve a lion's share of the responsibility. . . . The UFT (United Federation of Teachers) has committed a tremendous disservice to the entire teaching profession. More than that, it has created an atmosphere where people totally unsuited to deal with anybody's children have found permanent homes in teaching with good salaries and the protection of the system.

Mr. Vann's sentiments appealed to a significant number of low- and fixed-income people, especially his fellow activists at Oceanhill-Brownsville in the years 1968 and 1969. Welfare rights people responded to his call for unity and mutual cooperation. Within a few days of taking part in the school action, B-WAC's people were the most vocal group at the demonstration site. Shortly after that, welfare rights members began attending school-boycott planning meetings. The Oceanhill-Brownsville activist's efforts to negotiate a settlement with the teachers' union were rebuffed. Still, the school action proved that B-WAC members could function effectively in coalitions. Also, the adventure underscored organized clients' expanding interests.

Al Vann's arguments favoring the community's control of its institutions propelled B-WAC members into action on another front: the welfare centers. The issue — client control of the department, with administrators accountable to its constituents — represented a different way of thinking about the welfare system:

> We must get out and tell those community agencies what we are doing so when we are ready to take over they'll

stand with us. These agencies are the CACs, the Head Start centers, Settlement Houses, churches, parent associations, etc. We'll need their support because it will be us against the city this time. Before we were demanding something which the law said was our right. Now we are demanding what we say is our right and the Department is going to fight us harder and harder as they see us getting stronger.[33]

The proposal never received serious consideration by any nonwelfare rights groups, and members couldn't promote the changes alone. However, former WRO activists recalled that members found the idea fascinating and saw it as a goal to move toward.

There were additional, less publicized — but equally important — demonstrations. Recipients attempted to sell their blood in order to obtain money for school clothes. Three-quarters of the women were turned down because of poor health. Another action had B-WAC friends living for a week — some, for two weeks — on a welfare budget. At the end of the allotted time, these were some reactions:

> *Ms. Harrison*: I figured $57.20 and spent $54.31 for food and phone and transportation. The first week was an adventure but the second week fairly deadening. The three of us had colds, our morale was low. The kids wanted ginger ale and cookies but I couldn't afford them.
>
> *Ms. Sullivan, a caseworker*: I had to tell poverty mothers to spend only sixty-six cents a day on meals, and now I know better what it was like to experience this life.

Mr. Hanson, another advocate, commented that living on a welfare budget meant that he could not go out for a social evening or spend money for beer, take the kids to a ball game, or have fun.[34] In a quote from *Down and Out in the USA* by Lucy Komisar, a woman on welfare in 1972 puts the budget situation in perspective: "If you think that living on welfare is all sugar and honey, you're wrong because there is too much month left at the end of the money."35

AN OPPRESSIVE BANKING SYSTEM

Banks were problematic also. Manufacturers Hanover Trust (MHT) bank was known for its uncooperative tendencies toward clients, yet it handled the Welfare Department's account. Clients were required to patronize it or pay large fees to check-cashing stores. MHT confined recipients to one teller; and on days that checks were presented for payment, the line stretched outside and often around the block. Some branches assigned clients to entrances on the side streets or in alleys. These were life-threatening matters for clients, because in bad weather — regardless of season — weakened and undernourished clients could easily become ill. Drug and alcohol addicts preyed on the people in line, and muggings were frequent. Furthermore, bank staff were generally disrespectful to recipients.

B-WAC responded to members' complaints about this situation on two fronts: pressuring city officials to have the welfare account removed; and bargaining with bank staff regarding the elimination of discrimination against people on public assistance. B-WAC achieved some measure of success on the latter issue, but the agreements extended only to individual banks. Headquarters officials refused to meet with the activists. The campaign was a slow process and did not receive top priority at B-WAC.

INDIGENOUS VISTAs

There was one other major B-WAC experiment that did not fit the category of demonstrations. Still, it was an interesting experiment in grass roots control and empowerment. The regional office of VISTA approached B-WAC during 1969 with a proposal that it sponsor a VISTA program of neighborhood residents. VISTA Regional was particularly interested in recruiting B-WAC members, who would sign on for one year. In a move toward institutionalization, the membership agreed to sponsor and supervise 30 welfare-recipient VISTAs. All 18-year-old (or older) members of a B-WAC affiliate were eligible, provided they did not have any serious criminal records. For the B-WAC project, VISTA Regional waived its requirement disqualifying applicants with children under 18. B-WAC officers used the opportunity to fund B-WAC's current activities: mainly, recruitment and client advocacy at welfare centers and schools.

The project was relatively successful, if somewhat divisive because the 30 slots were insufficient for the large number of applicants. As is often the case, the applications of more well-known members were readily accepted. Indeed, active participants viewed the situation as a reward for their work. Straightaway, it became apparent that the client representatives in VISTA were expected by the community to conduct their duties in a conscientious manner by working long, late hours and being on call for any emergency; they were not a disappointment. Nonetheless, a small faction of jealous members emerged despite all efforts by the indigenous VISTAs to mollify them.

Any infractions of their responsibilities — a late arrival at a welfare center or meeting, say, or crossness with clients — would invite criticism from the resentful members. Regardless of these and other problems (to be detailed shortly), residents were generally proud of the community VISTAs; this attitude, in turn, increased the VISTA women's own self-respect. Essentially, they were the first "community mothers and sisters"[36] — accompanying people (mainly women) to clinics, hospitals, courts, and welfare centers, among other duties. Their responsibilities varied little from regular welfare rights organizing. But the title enhanced their image in the community.

The nature of the project fostered some bitterness and suspicion between grass roots leaders and the federal government. At the project's end, B-WAC and VISTA Regional had little or no genuine respect for one another. Their relationship reached a low point in June 1969, when a four-page unsigned letter critical of Regional (and attributed to a nonwelfare-rights Brooklyn VISTA official on the federal payroll) was circulated among local officials and B-WAC members. Questioning VISTA Regional's sincerity in helping low-income people to gain community power, the letter ended with an observation about its motives:

The volunteer must be left with the impression that VISTA's response to new ideas will be, at best, half-hearted. Again the program's success has been largely placed upon the volunteer without the same having control or meaningful opportunities to influence the implementation. As always, the people in our community become the real victim.[37]

Persistent rumors depicted Regional's true intentions as facilitating the development of informant systems throughout the country by way of indigenous VISTAs. The VISTA coordinator for Brooklyn, who was dissatisfied with the situation concerning the regional office, observed that

subterfuge and chicanery characterized NY Regional's acts. Aside from this, however, theirs has been a shabby record of deceit and hypocrisy.

Father Stevens described the problems in a 1983 interview:

In the era of community control aspirations, Regional VISTA officials' apparent reluctance to advance grass roots leadership through program administration, fostered mistrust and bitterness with the contract organization. The situation was exacerbated by lost or conflicting directives and memoranda, seemingly unnecessary requests for information and endless forms that needed to be completed; all of which resembled harassment of low income organizations.

Regardless of the discord between VISTA Regional and B-WAC, the latter was not in full accord with the letter of criticism, cited above. The experimental nature of the project combined with B-WAC's unorthodox activities could be expected to cause tensions, reasoned B-WAC members. Once B-WAC accepted the invitation to receive government funds, it was prepared for any eventuality. The program, however, was very important to members and the community. Most of the respondents in my study praised the indigenous VISTAs and were unaware of the disagreements between the regional VISTA office and B-WAC.

POLITICAL AND SOCIAL LOSSES

Near the end of 1968, New York State and City legal and social welfare policy recommendations threatening welfare rights gains were almost daily occurrences. One example is food stamps, which replaced surplus commodities despite strong opposition from the WROs. Most recipients opposed this program's enactment because using stamps pushed them further away from the mainstream. The use of stamps suggested that they could not be trusted to manage their funds. Similarly, recipients viewed food stamps as a giveaway to banks and supermarkets. The former received a fee to handle the stamps and therefore was gaining interest-free funds. The banks must have stood to increase their profits considerably with the welfare department's grant fund and the food stamp account. At the same time, supermarkets experienced an influx of customers with more captive buying power. Ms. Wise observed that "those stores operating in ghetto areas responded by raising prices."

Clients were limited in the items that they could buy. Deodorant, soap, detergent, toothpaste, and other nonfood items could not be purchased with food stamps. In contrast, the surplus commodities program provided low-income people with free flour and cornmeal, powdered milk and eggs, peanut butter, cheese, shortening, butter, Spam (a type of meat), canned goods, jelly, cereal, beans, and even occasionally whole peanuts and white sugar from the U.S. Department of Agriculture. With the creation of the food stamp program, these staples were discontinued. Program advocates believed that stamps would foster higher economic participation than surplus foods. Stamps, being less noticeable — advocates reasoned — would attract less stigma. Welfare rights opponents of the program countered by demanding a substantive raise in the regular monthly grants, thus making stamps as well as commodities unnecessary. In fact, both programs set poor people apart from society's mainstream, they argued. But at least commodities were free, varied, and plentiful. In that first year, food stamps required an up-front cash outlay,[38] and brought in less food than the surplus commodities provided. Therefore, clients' food-buying power decreased for two reasons: First, stamps required an expenditure not covered in the bimonthly welfare grant. Second, after buying stamps, less funds remained for nonfood items. The program was implemented over WRO objections before either advocates or opponents could fully realize the magnitude of the problems that it would bring.

After its enactment, B-WAC members utilized considerable energy to inform recipients about flaws in the food stamp program. Outraged customers stood in long, slow supermarket lines and watched items divided between money and stamps. Was soda pop or potato chips nonfood? Some clerks accepted stamps for everything; other cashiers bargained with the customer; while still others allowed only food and nonluxury items like soap and bathroom tissue to be purchased with stamps. Giving change was another problem. Some cashiers gave change in stamps; other clerks made change with money; and many others insisted that food stamp customers buy exact amounts, thereby eliminating change. Both clients and other customers disapproved of the situation, but it was the clients who took the brunt of verbal abuse from customers and employees. People were thrust into an untenable position with few alternatives. Food stamps exacerbated the problems that they were supposed to eliminate.

Another new program was proposed, and opposed by B-WAC. It required photographic identification cards in order to cash checks, receive medical services, or purchase food stamps. B-WAC objected on the ground that the picture identification — combined with the routine assigning of Social Security numbers to recipients' babies — violated civil rights. Further, the photo-identification contract was awarded to Polaroid — the company providing South Africa with the passbook pictures that it used as one stricture on its black majority population. Social Services officials maintained that check fraud and robbery were the reasons for instituting the system — points well taken, because these were serious issues in the community. Having lost or stolen checks replaced was a serious problem for clients. Initially, many unorganized clients welcomed the mandatory identification just as they did food stamps, because the programs had valid features. Once again, B-WAC activists had a double responsibility: to oppose the program and, simultaneously, to educate their constituents about its pitfalls.

> [Members] met with the Department of Welfare and bankers to hear about a photo identification card being the solution to the stolen checks problem. . . . Is someone in Goldberg's office worried about welfare recipients[?] No! It is because the mailmen were being robbed and they were threatening to stop carrying welfare checks. Also the insurance companies that used to guarantee payment to the banks that cash stolen welfare checks have cancelled their policies. . . . Citywide came up with the idea to solve the stolen check problem [with] a solution that would be just and not discriminatory. . . . The Department should deposit each client's monthly grant directly in a bank, open

a checking account in the client's name and treat us like any other checking customers.[39]

Both undertakings — opposing food stamps and the photo identification cards — proved difficult for the weary activists. Their gains diminished, while policies that they had determined were regressive were being introduced. After the productive years between 1967 and 1969, a former client leader described welfare rights advocacy in 1970 as "being in a pressure cooker." Ms. Carlye commented that "with political and social tensions building, blood pressure levels of many WRO activists climbed to unsafe levels, and their physicians ordered them to stay home." Nearly always in ill health even before this, the women deteriorated further. Medical problems — mental and physical — worsened as welfare rights power declined. These health concerns continue in the 1980s.

Lindsay's reform administration was defeated in 1974. Further welfare rights losses were demonstrated by the reinstatement of former Commissioner James Dumpson as head of the Department of Welfare. It was rumored that his assignment included removing sympathetic staff and implementing more stringent welfare policies. The circle was complete.[40]

B-WAC resisted the implementation of most programs that the department offered. Activists contended that the programs stigmatized clients, thus removing them further from the majority of Americans. For its part, the department believed that its proposals were addressing the concerns of recipients. In an environment that lacked communication between the two entities, conflicts were likely but also avoidable, observed an organizer. Input by organized clients should have been a department requisite in the conceptual stage of discussing programs. At that time, however, contacts between the Welfare Department and B-WAC members had virtually ended. B-WAC was about to close; and for all intents and purposes, the movement's demise had arrived. Pressure on the department to forge a dialogue with activists had waned.

Among other activities, in 1968 B-WAC spearheaded an

important voter education and registration drive. This action lacked sufficient funds and organization, but it had the potential to spur a large voting bloc. It could have delivered votes to any politician that requested its assistance. On the other hand, B-WAC didn't take itself seriously enough concerning politics. It was a sleeping giant, unaware or perhaps afraid of its own strength. Two candidates did ask the organization for its backing, and were refused. Members and B-WAC officers alike distrusted politicians, in part because the activists had limited electoral sophistication and because their historical experiences with politicians tended to be negative.[41] Most respondents now agree that the organization turned down a very special opportunity. Unwittingly, B-WAC participants rejected the chance to wage a significant, ongoing voter education and registration crusade—one that promised lasting empowerment.

B-WAC VICTORIES

Including those victories discussed earlier, the organization left a legacy of accomplishments and benefits for all recipients. To list the major ones: Caseworkers were required to provide written notice of their pending visits; and fair hearings were conducted and ruled on expeditiously, with the same being true for application for assistance. B-WAC pressure motivated the Welfare Department's release of carfare and—in many instances—lunch money to clients visiting welfare centers. Further—of major importance—the department instituted a procedure that informed recipients about entitlements and rights, on a continuing basis. Caseworker–client personal contacts were conducted in a more professional manner. B-WAC's most significant codicil were the recipients' newly acquired feelings of hope for the future and a new sense of joining America. Those attitudes were still evident in my 1985 interviews with respondents, but former leaders believe that their sons and daughters are more cynical—even hostile—about the state of

Black America in the 1980s. Yet the young people are ambitious and hopeful about the future. Important questions gained a public hearing due to B-WAC activities.

Even if the questions call for open ended answers, the very fact of asking the question focuses . . . attention on issues that we might not normally care about.[42]

A new consciousness – developed by organized clients – was thrust on welfare recipients and other citizens alike. It fostered the notion that persons receiving public assistance have hopes, dreams, and goals similar to those of nonrecipients. Welfare rights organizing removed the layers of myths and enabled financially secure people to see recipients' strengths in addition to their universal problems. Women on welfare – almost all of whom were single parents – organized for benefits and improvements in their lives, working with only limited recognition from the media, feminists, and civil rights organizations. "But the legacy they left others," commented a respondent, "is a symbolic applause for their efforts."

In the end, B-WAC members attempted to gain access to the mainstream, while refusing co-optation. They tried to avoid the case-by-case approach to service – that is, where the advocate assists with individual matters and changes the person to fit the system, which can be a 20-hour-a-day effort, so massive are the problems.[43] Regarding individual assistance, they capitulated and helped as many individuals as possible. But this type of activity left no room for addressing the larger issues, from which case-by-case difficulties stem. On the other hand, organizing and politicizing people on a mass scale – while vital – would leave individual crises intact. Recipients, who were experiencing almost daily emergencies, required immediate succor. Therefore, members had to respond individually, because they too were recipients and knew the full consequences of emergencies.

As B-WAC became more establishment oriented, its leaders

understood the magnitude of the welfare system's strength and pliability. This realization occurred as many leaders were entering a period of burnout and diminishing altruistic motives. The future offered at least three options for the organization: to close its doors, revise its objectives, or bureaucratize its activities. B-WAC principals chose the first alternative, and ended operations in the fall of 1971.

ADDITIONAL ISSUES: MOBILIZATION, COALITION BUILDING, AND DEPENDENCY

An examination of the Brooklyn experience raises questions about poor people's movements in general. Can we reject the fact that class and gender distortions exist, regarding the mobilization versus organization theory? Considering that women constitute much of the poverty class, is it reasonable to assume that they would be the majority among those participating in any social or economic change effort? If that is the case, then their needs must be identified and must receive priority when organizing plans are developed.

Poor women even in urban settings are often as isolated as their rural (and suburban) counterparts. Thus, a movement that encompasses mobilization as well as membership organization would be effective provided that friendships, support systems, and shared nurturing were its foundation. Women often respond more readily to such an approach; thus, it could attract the requisite middle class, which would be primarily females because they constitute the bulk of volunteers. The Brooklyn groups employed some aspects of this strategy, although much of their coalition building and networking languished because the members did not appreciate the importance of alliances while the priests were still participating. Once the church men left, the need for a strong B-WAC Friends of Welfare Rights (FWRO) group became apparent.

To some degree, the clergy must share the blame in this matter. The priests had established a friendship network that contributed seed money, furniture, and equipment, among other items. However, that system was weak since it collapsed when the priests ended their welfare rights involvement in 1970. To have begun serious coalition building at that point — with the city administration becoming more traditional — would have been unrealistic, and probably would have consumed more energy than the members could rally.

It was at this stage that the members at last understood the complexity and consequences of their status subordinate to the Catholic church. As one interviewee said, "[One] should always be in a position of not being anchored to one agency who in turn could pull the strings.[44] How much influence could a friends' group exert on the Brooklyn Catholic diocese? And if the role of the friends had been very substantial, wouldn't B-WAC simply have exchanged dependency from one group to the other? Economic independence is the only sure way out of this dilemma. How to obtain funds and maintain independence is an age-old question.

Specifically — subordination is another critical variable here. Destroying that syndrome was one of B-WAC's primary goals because its members had to contend with socialized inferiority as females and institutionalized subordination by the Welfare Department. One could maintain that institutional dependency and subordination expanded through the participation of another influential entity, the Catholic church. It is possible that some forms of dependency can be positive,[45] but only when a group is sufficiently influential to parry any attacks on its autonomy. Welfare rights participants lacked prominent supporters, aside from the Catholic church. Consequently, like most grass roots organizations, its defenselessness gave it only a short — but noteworthy — life span.

SOCIAL PLANNERS AS FACILITATORS

Mobilization strategy inspires numerous questions: Who authorizes it, and who are the negotiators during and after the action—professionals or indigenous leaders? How is the momentum sustained? Mobilizing to disrupt bureaucracies is the logical strategy for nonestablishment citizens according to Cloward and Piven. Aside from disruption, poor people's influence is minuscule, they observed. Welfare recipients and other poor people have no powerful backers or organizations with ample resources to support their concerns. To a limited degree, William Gamson supports Cloward and Piven's mobilization theory:

Sponsorship is an indicator of a privileged group . . . and an affluent member may wheel and deal but a challenger should be prepared to stand and fight. If a group threatens strong interests of powerholders and is not ready for combat, it is likely to find itself extremely vulnerable to attack and defeat.[46]

Social planners will be the ones responsible for assisting in the promotion of solutions to questions concerning mobilization or organization of grass roots people. Social planners are pragmatists and organizers, and—at the same time—have the skills to conduct sociological research. They could assist community leaders in designing actions and demonstrations that would have maximum impact. To achieve economic parity, social change must take new directions and approaches. All the former B-WAC members, staff, organizers, even James Farmer agreed that the absence of substantive planning in the movement was among the reasons that its success was limited.[47] This may sound contradictory in that the member-recipients were struggling to acquire self-confidence and independence, and needed the assistance of white (and black) professionals to promote expansion and growth within B-WAC. And given the climate of increasing black nationalism in most 1960s civil rights organizations, the conflict concerning sources of ideas and direction may appear more pronounced than it was. It must be understood that whites were always welcome in the Brooklyn welfare rights organization. Its members resented authority more than race or class. Social planners would have been welcomed so long as they were willing to accept criticism and ideas, use grass roots strategies, and share power. The movement needed professionals from other disciplines, with substantive — but less traditional — skills. A coalition of community and professional activists could have made a long-term positive contribution by assisting with the institutionalization of B-WAC. Indeed, it can be argued that planners have the moral and professional obligation to reaffirm their role as futurists by undertaking some difficult tasks regarding politically disadvantaged people.

In doing so, they could demonstrate to middle- and upper-class people, the relatedness of lower income community actions to the overall quality of life in the United States. The case can be made that short-lived class benefits at poor people's expense yield long-term problems so catastrophic that coming generations pay a terrible price. Simultaneously, planners should consider themselves precursors of the activist professionals in assisting grass roots initiatives. Planners may be interested in drafting and offering alternatives that will support current social and economic strengths as well as eliminate the weaknesses. In addition, we can broaden our horizons by adopting strategies for change that emanate from those most needful of social change. There is truth to the contention that the process for social and economic improvements is in the minds of people on the bottom. In partnership with social planners, the insight of the poor can be utilized for everyone's benefit.

This analysis of B-WAC's strategies and motivations is one planner's attempt to implement the second component of planning for social change. Facilitating responses to issues and developing indigenous leaders to participate in the design, administration, or establishment of programs and community institutions are the primary objectives of this phase. The effort can be carried out by nurturing community residents' confidence and by stressing the worth of grass roots ideas and strategies. Phase one—advocacy—essentially embraces the concept of providing technical assistance to grass roots organizations. The formulation of questions, philosophy, and strategies remain in the professionals' domain (not necessarily the planning professional). Lower income community groups have had a degree of programmatic success with this model. Phase two—facilitation—is the natural outgrowth of the advocacy endeavor. In addition, planners could serve as community brokers. Poor people's social and economic improvement ventures can be made less difficult and more effective by putting sympathetic and influential contacts in place for them.

When B-WAC closed, the WROs essentially disappeared. Its members scattered, yet they are still basically active. Given this core of seasoned community activists, I cannot help wondering whether a similar—but more establishment-type— organization could have been established, with the assistance of the appropriate professionals. In discussions concerning B-WAC's demise, 14 of the 17 former WRO leaders agreed that this might have been so. One expressed no opinion, due to her bitter memories of welfare rights and B-WAC. Another dissenting leader, Ms. Samuels, believed that "Recipients were sophisticated enough to steer the organization in a new direction, if funds had been available."[48] One final member was unsure what—if anything—would be useful in new efforts for social change. Chapter 6 will address this issue and offer recommendations.

NOTES

   1. However, B-WAC's expenditures increased sixfold when it was conducting leadership training classes (which will be subsequently discussed)— peaking at $33,000 in 1969. Some financial records were kept by Catholic Charities on these specific expenditures.
   2. From the author's interview with Hulbert James in 1982, New York City.
   3. Rhoda Linton was an important player in B-WAC's formation and success. A firm believer in community control and grass roots empowerment,

she left the council once it had passed its infancy.

4. Only welfare recipients could hold offices in the council.

5. Andrea Kydd, the new staff member, replaced Rhoda Linton, who had convinced B-WAC members that it was time for her to leave and that her replacement must be a person of color.

6. Rhoda Linton, B-WAC acting coordinator, and Ezra Birnbaum, a labor organizer, were the authors of the leadership development curriculum.

7. From "B-WAC Memorandum Re: Leadership Training Project Proposal," January 18, 1968.

8. From one of the author's 20 interviews with former B-WAC leaders, in 1982.

9. Observation made during a summer 1982 interview with Ms. Howard, a former WRO leader.

10. From the author's interview with a former welfare rights leader, in the spring of 1982. Emphasis added.

11. NWRO's executive director, the late George Wiley, recruited the B-WAC president and public relations director for assignment at the national office in Washington, D.C. These women, both single parents, were the first former welfare recipients on the NWRO staff.

12. Norman Fainstein and Susan Fainstein, *Urban Political Movements* (Englewood Cliffs, N.J.: Prentice-Hall, 1974), p. 198.

13. Ibid., p. 177.

14. For an extensive discussion of this issue, read Marilyn Gittell and Theresa Shtob, "Changing Women's Roles in Political Volunteerism and Reform of the City," *Signs: Journal of Women in Culture and Society* 5, 3 (1980).

15. Richard Cloward and Frances Fox Piven, *Poor People's Movements: Why They Succeed, How They Fail* (New York: Vintage Books, 1979), p. 296.

16. Mitchell Svirdoff was interviewed in 1983 at his New York City office.

17. The Citywide Coordinating Council of Welfare Rights Groups (Citywide), which included representatives from all boroughs, decided to increase its lobbying and meetings with welfare officials—over Brooklyn's objections. Although informed when meetings were scheduled, the representatives from Brooklyn often decided against attending. During this time, Brooklyn was planning a massive credit drive that involved staging disruptions inside the borough's well-known department stores. This and other actions are described in the text.

18. See Cloward and Piven *Poor People's Movements* for a detailed study of disruptive tactics.

19. William A. Gamson, *The Strategy of Social Protest* (Homewood, Ill.: Dorsey Press, 1975), pp. 65 and 142.

20. An example is the campaign by B-WAC for a National guaranteed

annual income (GAI). See Chapter 4.

21. Many social movement theorists have placed much significance on self-serving behavior, yet the women in B-WAC as well as other welfare rights groups quickly submerged self-interest to further the larger community's cause. Moreover, this phenomenon is most common among female activists, regardless of class. Eric Hirsch's unpublished 1984 report, "The Creation of Political Solidarity in Social Movement Organizations : A Critique of the Resource Mobilization Approach," p. 19, supports—to some degree—this observation : "In the third and final stage of the mobilization process, individuals submerge their individual interests in a larger group interest, that is, group goals become their goals. Self-sacrifice in pursuit of these emergent group interests seems to be relatively common." Self-sacrifice—to which women are already socialized—begins almost with the decision to join a group.

22. Untitled and unsigned article, *Tablet*, July 16, 1968.

23. Hulbert James, director of Citywide, in the New York *Times*, August 14, 1968.

24. Martin Morganstein, president of the Social Service Employers Union of Case Workers, in the New York *Post*, August 14, 1968.

25. New York *Post*, August 14, 1968.

26. Robert Carroll, special assistant to the welfare commissioner, in the New York *Times*, August 14, 1968.

27. The utility companies' community relations (CR) departments gained new prominence as a result of the opposition campaigns conducted by various community groups. Companies and corporations whose public relations units had primarily served the media quickly hired CR specialists as negotiators with grass roots groups. The trend provided first-time corporate employment for scores of middle-class people of color. This is an illustration of the benefits that middle-income people obtained from welfare recipients' activities.

28. In January 1969, WROs throughout the United States demonstrated at selected retail establishments for credit, while NWRO leaders opened negotiations with Montgomery Ward and Sears, Roebuck and Co. The former agreed to a $100 credit line for NWRO members, while Sears maintained its opposition to the proposal.

29. The Friends of Welfare Rights Organization (FWRO) was a group of professional, mainly white, middle-class or wealthy individuals sympathetic to the plight and goals of welfare clients. They contributed time and money to the movement. Further, FWRO members made contacts and frequently spoke on behalf of WROs at various functions. Almost every welfare rights group (local, state, and national)—except B-WAC—organized FWROs. In most cases, FWRO members were not permitted to hold

office or vote. Many staff organizers – particularly the late George Wiley – disagreed with this regulation. They felt that FWRO participants could be useful in expanding WRO to include middle-class activists – for example, white feminists and environmentalists.

30. I have used quotes to designate role-playing B-WAC members.

31. Brooklyn's Oceanhill-Brownsville demonstration school district (for community control) – funded by the Ford Foundation – split New York City. The issues of contention ranged from community control of all institutions teaching African-American history and culture to charges of racism and anti-Semitism. Like the rest of the city, the Jewish community split on the issues, with young Jewish educators crossing strike lines of their parents and other relatives. At the request of the African-American community, the strike breakers kept many of the schools open. Most parents noticed an increase in their children's reading level during this upheaval, observed several respondents. They attributed this phenomenon to the dedication of the young Jewish teachers. Al Vann played a major role in that strike; the resulting publicity became his vehicle for entering politics (see the text below and note 32).

32. Al Vann was a popular and controversial teacher as well as president of the African-American Teachers Association, founder and chairman of the Vannguard Civic Association, and a member of Community School Board #13. Today – in 1988 – Vann is a representative in the New York State Legislature and continues to be an important leader in the black community. Efforts to interview him proved fruitless.

33. Sherrell Covian, "Steps to Control Welfare Centers," *Welfare Righter*, March 28, 1969.

34. These three people were part of a similar action developed by the New York State Welfare Rights Organization (NYS-WRO).

35. Lucy Komisar, *Down and Out in the USA: A History of Social Welfare* (New York: New Viewpoints, 1974), p. ii.

36. A current (beginning in 1981) teenage-parent service program called Project Redirection is operating in Harlem; it provides young women with a community mother to assist them in their efforts to manage their lives better.

37. The letter was returned to its original owner, a former WRO leader.

38. By 1988, food stamps were provided without charge to public welfare recipients.

39. Nannette Beecham, "Your Picture to Combat Organized Crime," *Welfare Righter*, March 28, 1969.

40. James R. Dumpson had been welfare commissioner in 1964, and his administration had not been renowned for progressive initiatives. For example, the infamous midnight raids – abolished in 1966 by Ginsberg –

flourished during Dumpson's first tenure. (See Chapter 3).

41. Major Owens, Al Vann, and other, less noteworthy Brooklyn political activists did receive the support of individual welfare recipients. Politicians or activists who had strong potential and endorsements from other grass roots organizations could and did secure clients' admiration and energy.

42. Roberta Ash Garner, *Social Change* (Chicago: Rand McNally, 1977).

43. Disillusioned and frustrated, some leaders left to work for the establishment — "feeling like we had joined the enemy," said Ms. Wise.

44. From the author's July 1982 interview with former client activists, in Brooklyn, New York.

45. In the late nineteenth century, working-class white women formed working girls' clubs "out of a simple desire for companionship and self-improvement," with the financial responsibilities of the group assumed by sympathetic upper-middle-class women. Admittedly, in 1900 the elite dominated the decision-making roles; but by "1901 eighty percent of officers in twenty-one New York City clubs were working class." Excerpted from Joanne Reitano, "Working Girls Unite," *American Quarterly* 36 (Spring 1984): 112–34.

46. Gamson, *Strategy of Protest*, pp. 65 and 142. See Cloward and Piven, *Poor People's Movements*.

47. In a speech before the Humanist Society in 1985, James Farmer, former CORE chairman, asserted that the "absence of a plan" was the single most important reason that the civil rights movement ended.

48. From an August 1982 interview conducted by the author in Brooklyn, New York.

6

Summary, Findings, and Recommendations

We never received welfare — that word means well-being and security. All we ever got was handouts, given in the most degrading inhumane way possible.[1]

In Brooklyn during the 1960s, a group of women receiving public assistance challenged traditional views of poverty and demanded structural changes in the institution of social welfare. During a four-year period, they mobilized thousands of recipients in the struggle for special grants and welfare rights. Furthermore, the women established and administered a social change vehicle: the Brooklyn Welfare Action Council. The only organization managed by welfare clients, it became the largest of its kind in New York State, and its members constituted more than one-third of the National Welfare Rights Organization.

Brooklyn's welfare rights movement essentially followed the pattern of most lower economic class protests. Lacking large numbers of influential, wealthy supporters or acceptance by the majority society, it lasted just a few years. As with similar organizations, B-WAC's momentum was impossible to maintain. Thus, when demonstrations, mobilization, and recruitment efforts were curtailed, it lost members. The reasons that this situation developed are numerous and complex. Among them is the disillusionment of members regarding their ability to reach the long-range goal of a guaranteed annual income. The social and economic environment eventually assumed a more traditional posture and was less accepting of unconventional organizations, while the city government staff shifted its emphasis accordingly. Fifteen of the former client leaders agreed with my assessment that welfare rights members were then left with difficult and limited options: They could endure and continue the program of demonstrations and mobilization, and invite more arrests. They could reconsider and change their initial objectives—namely, modification of the welfare system and the development of grass roots leadership. Or they could cease operations. Just two interviewees believed that demonstrations had been critical for recruiting—that they should have been continued, and even increased.

Regarding the revision of long-term goals (presumably as a result of members' discussions), these could have developed into strategies for an underground movement with covert activities. All former leaders indicated that B-WAC participants never did consider such an alternative. They elected to keep inviolate the original goals, but abandon disruptive tactics and instead build an institution through which to promote social change. The latter endeavor failed, because members lacked the skills to accomplish it. Organizers were split and unhappy with B-WAC's decision. Two wanted the mobilization strategy to continue. Nevertheless, in a 1984 interview with the author, Frances Fox Piven agreed that interminable mobilization was unrealistic. She admitted that poor people's unions or groups should establish modest bureaucracies. But Professor Piven cautioned that, when organizations imitate middle-class associations, they operate against poor people's interests. Grass roots institutions need a flexibility and innovativeness that reflect community needs.

The infusion of new ideas and recruits often ceases while

long-time members consolidate their own power. An excessive amount of organizational energy may be used in lobbying for support, noted Piven. A major component of lobbying is negotiation – and what do poor people have to negotiate with except their numbers? – she asked rhetorically, maintaining her position that poor people's greatest social-change strategy will always be street demonstrations.[2] Whether that specific option or any of the others listed above were reasonable techniques for B-WAC may be determined by a brief re-examination of its participants and their lives.

Providing new opportunities for their children was the members' fundamental concern, since many believed it was too late for them (although that view proved to be false) – according to the 17 respondents. Anger at a system that they perceived as unjust – followed by the refusal, as Ms. Samuel stated, "to take any more abuse"[3] – impelled the participants. Support and admiration for the southern civil-rights demonstrations was certainly a contributing factor. Moreover, the Catholic church had a major role in shaping members' goals and the direction of the movement. The nuns' and priests' intervention helped to channel suppressed energies into constructive activities.

One laudable result of the clients' anger and organized efforts is that most of the former leaders who consented to interviews have left the welfare rolls. Of the 17 leaders interviewed, 15 are no longer receiving public assistance. All returned to and completed high school. Four now have college credits, and two have their master of arts degrees. None of the leaders' sons and daughters are recipients (except one grandchild whose father was in prison at the time of the interview). The children too are high school graduates; and most were in college full-time in 1982–83, or working and attending college part-time. Said one respondent,

My children and I were fortunate; our progression has been slow but steady. In 1985 my newly built house in Mississippi will be completely furnished. I'll return with my youngest child and live out my life on the land left to me by my father.[4]

The composition of B-WAC's membership brought enthusiasm to an organization that few expected would be effective. Its uniqueness stemmed from the participation of nonsalaried, middle-age women of color who were single parents. They created a movement of people thought to be unorganizable, and who had been designated the lumpen proletariat by some intellectuals and activists. Essentially, B-WAC was a grass-roots women's union, although the members were outside the labor force and alienated from their natural allies. The movement was a priori establishment oriented, and traditional in many respects – but gradationally progressive as it achieved a degree of political maturity. Participants did succeed in implementing a training program and in developing community leaders.

Despite the movement's demise, former members persist in confronting issues that impact negatively on poor people's lives. In 1988 they can be found working for many community causes including block associations, school and planning boards, welfare recipient councils, and political clubs.

Would these women have accomplished as much without the welfare rights movement? Were they the fittest welfare clients, and therefore programmed for a better life? Respondents maintain that they could not have obtained any real measure of success without welfare rights. However, the second question requires an ambiguous answer – yes and no. Yes, the members were the best. Presumably, the more downtrodden welfare clients remained at home – inactive. Nonetheless, even those who stayed home received new benefits because of B-WAC members' activities.

In all probability, the lives of the members would have stagnated had they, too, decided against participating. At the very least, their circumstances would have been far harsher than they are at the present time. The women and their children might have continued in the ranks of helpless people – with life's enthusiasm essentially buried, and all hope extinguished by the weight of poverty's burdens. The respondents in my study asserted that B-WAC members had inspired many people and had supported an endeavor bent on eliminating the barriers of poverty and despair. Ms. Hamburg said,

It [WRO] helped me come out of my shell, meet new people and overcome shyness. I've traveled, done public speaking, obtained a high school diploma, a B.A. as well as an M.A. from Adelphi University.[5]

For their part, the church women and men who were B-WAC's main organizers facilitated traditional concepts, despite some antimainstream sentiment. Politically and religiously progressive, these activists helped many people in their efforts to enhance the quality of their lives within the confines of the system. They pushed members beyond the restrictions set by themselves and by the Welfare Department. With this encouragement, clients realized that some limitations were flexible and could expand—enabling them to improve their lives. The clergy's efforts and methods during that era have and will influence subsequent organizers' and theorists' concepts of grant-income people. Their doctrine was that of helping others to help themselves, and of developing indigenous leadership, combined with a fundamental respect and belief in the worthiness of every individual.

The priest taught me that the system is the problem—not the people. For the first time in my life someone was telling me I'm a worthy human being. Welfare Rights organizing made me feel I could do almost anything I wanted to do. The priest talked with me and explained politics, classism, etc.[6]

To strengthen and enhance family life was the clergy's primary goal. The priests and nuns labored to expand community services through establishing neighborhood storefront classes. In short, they concentrated their efforts on guiding welfare recipients into the cultural and economic mainstreams, believing that grant-income people would be assets to the community. To accomplish these fundamental goals, the clergy organized people on welfare for the purpose of negotiating with the system to increase benefits for those persons entitled to receive them.

Their social change philosophy differed from that of Cloward and Piven. These two theorists advocated eliminating or reforming the system, thereby ensuring that services would be more responsive to users. Both sets of approaches were correct as well as successful in the 1960s for the populations with whom the academicians and the clergy worked.

Self-help activities by the members—the approach used by the clergy—resulted in increased individual efforts to sever the ties of dependence. The priests' idealistic but pragmatic concept for ending poverty altered and enhanced the lives of individuals and families. On the other hand, the theorists concentrated on raising the consciousness of America regarding the welfare system's inequities, by way of mobilizing clients. Which social change approach was more effective and provided long-term results? Both, must be the response for now, pending any future B-WAC research.

FORMER ORGANIZERS AND STAFF IN THE 1980s

After Fathers Stevens and Matthews left the welfare rights movement, they followed careers in health and education that offered avenues of continued advocacy for the politically disenfranchised. Their life styles are as unpretentious in 1988 as in 1969.[7] Also the former staff's current positions are comparable to those of the clergy. Employed primarily by nonprofit agencies, their advocacy has moved from the streets to less radical activities. Yet, 20 years later, their views and life styles have changed little. Many staff in similar welfare rights groups as well as other movements secured prominent positions once their activism ended. And members of those groups usually embraced a life style that precluded any renewed community participation. For B-WAC members, however, community activism endures. They have not gained substantial financial benefits, although most are aspiring middle class — particularly the grown daughters and sons.

That welfare rights groups existed at all demonstrates that women on welfare were willing to struggle for a better quality of life, despite mainstream perceptions of them as uncaring mothers who were content with public assistance. Fostering changes in local and national social policies, grant-income individuals along with a few middle-class people responded to the welfare rights challenge and counted themselves more psychologically complete as a result of that experience.

Finally, the changing nature of the organization and of the political climate facilitated a typical move toward institutionalization of the welfare movement. The closing of B-WAC's doors can be viewed as a tribute to its original concepts and objectives, because its members refused establishment demands for conformity to a system that was oppressive to them.

At the same time, one could argue that shutting down may have illustrated the need for new professionals in welfare rights who were not of the mobilization–disruption genre. Their absence impeded the movement's natural progression to its next stage. For instance, some adoption of establishment strategies — strengthened by welfare rights precepts and goals — was inevitable, admitted respondents, but members did not have access to different opinions. At that stage of development, they would have welcomed fresh initiatives and approaches. Accordingly, the organization's natural move to the next level was thwarted because members' decisions were limited to narrow alternatives. In other words, how informed were the members' decisions in the last days of B-WAC?

For one thing, participants remained opposed to delegating

decision-making to nonrecipients; yet they lacked the necessary skills to function in a changed social and political environment. Brooklyn Catholic Charities, for example, discontinued its funding of B-WAC because it was part of the rising conservative trend across the country. With its social brokers gone, WRO leaders were stunned and unprepared to respond. Outsiders bearing credentials moved in to manage the community organizations. Some of them disregarded grass roots strategies or contributions. The philosophy of community participation was finished, as well as the opportunity for shared program planning. Institutions with indigenous administrators were no longer fundable, and the community was the real loser.

SOCIAL CHANGE PLANNING MODEL AND ISSUES

This research still leaves many questions unanswered. Let us consider one of them: Does the Brooklyn experience fit an urban social-planning model? First of all, a short description of the planning process itself becomes necessary. The planning process is an attempt at orderly development for achieving given objectives. It offers a series of general guides to future decisions and actions. This intellectual process — as opposed to action in the form of fact finding and gathering, statistical compilation, demonstrations, and negotiating — can be characterized as the following steps:

1. goals and priorities clarification to determine the relevant facts, social and political realities, and trends;
2. taking inventory of the available and obtainable knowledge, skills, and resources;
3. discovering and analyzing alternative directions in addition to predicting the outcomes;
4. formal agreement on expressed preferences and a choice process;

5. translating policies into programs; and
6. continually evaluating program outcomes.[8]

We can now determine the extent to which B-WAC members employed — or related to — these concepts. Following the aforementioned steps — interspersed with action — the organized clients developed advocacy guidelines for themselves that could be adopted by subsequent participants and movement theorists. But as we shall witness, their major weakness was in neglecting steps four and six.

Formal agreement on preferences for the future or on goals was lacking. Perhaps the organizers/priests were unaware of the need to identify common objectives. Or possibly they assumed that everyone involved was working under an implicit agreement. If participants had any initial misgivings about options, they ignored them once their achievements began to multiply. As B-WAC matured and political attacks on it increased, thoughts of common goal-setting faded and were replaced by efforts to survive. During the interviews for this research, every member except one (and she had no opinion) complained that their preferences for the future had not been elicited — which, according to social protest theorists, is similar to other movements.

In the interviews, the welfare rights leaders and the clergy both agreed unanimously that determining and analyzing alternatives had been lacking in their organizing model. Save for the general consent concerning a guaranteed annual income, no one discussed choices or prepared clients for possible failure — again, a general weakness of poor people's groups. Neither in B-WAC classes nor programmatically were members advised that bureaucratic retrenchment could develop, bringing dire consequences. As James Farmer said in a 1985 speech: "Poor people's organizations dealt with daily crises. They had no time to develop a plan."[9]

Indeed, when the retrenchment began, participants felt lost and unsuited for the new challenge. Had there been continuing analysis and discussion of the movement's future, that particular organizational flaw would have surfaced and been addressed. Similarly, the "next step" to which all the member respondents referred in the interviews would have emerged out of debates on alternatives. Given B-WAC's history of member participation in decision-making, this oversight was totally uncharacteristic. Had members been offered truly equal status within the policy planning and development process, it is likely that the Brooklyn movement could have taken a different route and actually prolonged the institution's existence.

At the very minimum, contributing to the process of steps four and six would have furthered members' personal coping abilities and empowerment. With these two important elements of the planning technique missing, activists experienced a sense of anomie, and they turned inward—for a time, shunning each other or even squabbling—when B-WAC ceased to function. Fortunately, that period was short lived, but it was certainly typical of organizations on the wane.

As a result of strengths enhanced by participating in the movement, the former members were able to enter the human rights struggle in other arenas with the same or new colleagues. Nevertheless, an avoidable breach developed between once trusting and mutually respecting people, compounded by a period of self-imposed isolation along with loss of contact. Is it any wonder that—as interviewees confided to me—in the aftermath of B-WAC they felt lonely, abandoned, and used by people for whom they had a great deal of admiration?

A stronger support system would have been useful at this stage of their lives. The majority of the members had become acquainted at B-WAC, and were novices at networking. Inevitably, their fragile networks floundered. Old friends and family "picked up the pieces," said Ms. Delta, one of the former welfare rights leaders; but many of these people offered limited sympathy and nurturing. They chided the welfare activists for being too gullible, saying, "I told you so."[10] Thus—back home again and basically alone—welfare rights women had made a full circle.

Inversely, the clergy did recognize the need and importance of a support system, and maintained close ties with each other. Their friendships had been forged in precollege and undergraduate years. In fact, here may be the reason for the ignoring of those two planning steps: the priests' closeness. They had their own common preferences and goals, which were not shared with members. It is even likely that informal evaluations of WRO activities were being discussed within their old-boys network of church and school friends.

Planning theorists and practitioners can acquire much knowledge by continuing research on the Brooklyn Welfare Action Council. It can contribute to social science by shedding new light on planning's role in community and grass roots organizing, while illustrating the importance of adhering to the planning process. Further, an examination of B-WAC reinforces the notion that planning is and should be ingrained into daily operations.

Without such planning – as we have shown – issues remain submerged for long periods and surface only during organizational crisis. At those times, the social change effort faces possible destruction from within. Poor peoples' unions are fragile instruments; accordingly, every conceivable obstacle or variable must be identified and planned for. No operational or administrative variable of a low-income organization can be overlooked. Be it a civic or purely social group, a low-income organization is a potentially political social change venture and must be treated as such.

Power holders are ever alert and suspicious when poor men and women look beyond basic survival issues and form a collective of future activists, while planners at the community level are also held suspect by the influential institutions of society. Progressive social planners – as futurists with bureaucratic credentials and acceptability – have the nearly impossible task of maintaining the community activist group's viability; and this is not an enviable job. We planners may be hesitant about offering our services to grass roots people because the commitment will likely be a major one, and the task arduous—often thankless. Still, concerned planners must look into the future honestly and acknowledge that continued social-political inequities will surely end in upheavals throughout the nation. We can assist those searching for less painful solutions, or remain part of the problem. Assuming that the former choice is the more acceptable and logical one to embrace, it is incumbent on us—working with community input—to develop processes and programs that promote indigenous leadership and encompass progressive thinking among grass-roots and grant-income people.

In sum, the findings suggest that:

— recipients of public assistance (like all poor people's groups) organized to obtain benefits to improve the quality of their lives and the lives of their families, and to fully participate in the mainstream of society.

— B-WAC's strengths included imparting precepts of self-respect and confidence to its members through training, sharing, and confronting the issues that welfare clients face, and through its political awareness classes. Its weaknesses encompassed its inability to institutionalize, or to promote its constituents' interests using mainstream vehicles enriched by grass roots strategies and concepts. In these respects, it was almost identical to other poor people's movements.

— the members held politically and socially traditional views, which may have conflicted with the movement's theorists.

— future goals were unclear to the members, but were shared among the organizers, theorists, and staff.

— the movement had local impact on social policy especially in the areas of credit for grant-income people, and utility companies' policies. It had national influence in concert with other welfare rights groups by acting as a catalyst for public debate on the flaws in the welfare system, and by proposing a guaranteed national income for everyone.

— the organization/mobilization debate continues without a definitive resolution. Of the 39 interviewees in my study, 36 believed that building a strong organization would have been a viable approach to sustaining social change activities.

— in order to enhance their efforts to meet the needs of a disenfranchised population, social planners can simulate alternative grass-roots techniques in the design and implementation of social programs.

In many respects, B-WAC differed little from other poor people's movements — being short lived, with its most active members joining the mainstream and the majority of welfare clients making only limited personal advancement. But organized clients did come out of the proverbial closet; and despite scorn from most other groups — particularly from uninformed welfare recipients — they made social gains and achieved an increased measure of self-respect and confidence. In the truest sense of the word, they were "minorities" five times over — being economically disadvantaged; women of color, and ethnics; middle age; recipients of public aid; and (many of them) fat.

Mobilization and organization are the two approaches that together will advance social change for low- and grant-income people, according to the evidence and according to the respondents' views. Client leaders understood that sustained mobilization was unrealistic. An organization employing some middle-class concepts while continuing its grass roots initiatives was necessary for B-WAC's existence, they reasoned. Cloward and Piven essentially agreed with the leaders on that issue, but they would organize on a more limited scale. The two theorists admitted that some organization would advance poor people's interests, but maintained that mobilization is the primary approach to strengthening the causes of low-income and grant-income people.

But putting aside that debate, another critical feature in welfare rights was the joint effort of black and white, middle and lower economic people — using the resources of two powerful institutions, religious and academic — to enhance the quality of life in the United States by raising issues of personal, social, and economic equity for national discussion and scrutiny. This resulted in pressure on government to increase benefits and services to the poor. Public agencies bowed to the mandate — but reluctantly. Now, in 1988, administrators must continue the initiatives begun by those public activists by at least keeping the doors of change open. In this era, it is incumbent on people who believe that change is possible from within — especially social planners — to renew and realize WRO's goals.

The advocacy planning stage has matured; and we as change catalysts in the twenty-first century can be in the forefront of creating an atmosphere that fosters the expansion of democracy through respect for the ideas of all Americans, including the very poor. Fundamental freedoms must not be limited to people with access to the power holders.

I learned, I am somebody. Welfare Rights meant a right to life — it freed me from emotional slavery. I am a person you can't push aside; I have the right to be. Welfare Rights showed me that my counterparts are all around; knowing this, I no longer feel alone. Welfare Rights lives — me and other people are still active, struggling for a better life. PTAs, school boards, even political clubs have former WR's members and we continue pushing the welfare rights agenda.[11]

B-WAC lives in the minds of everyone remotely associated with it. An organization for and by poor people, a women's movement that addressed real survival issues. Its concepts and promises live in us and our children.[12]

NOTES

1. Ms. Raysmer, a welfare rights leader who died in 1987, made this comment in a 1984 interview with the author. She was a single parent of five

sons and daughters, four of whom have finished at least two years of college. Raysmer herself was a high school dropout.

2. From the author's fall 1984 interview with Frances Fox Piven, in New York City.

3. From the author's summer 1982 interview with Evelyn Samuel in Brooklyn, New York.

4. From the author's 1983 interview with a former leader-client, in Brooklyn, New York.

5. From the author's summer 1983 interview with a former leader-client, in Brooklyn, New York.

6. From the author's interview in the summer of 1982 with a former leader-client in Brooklyn, New York.

7. All but two of the former priests and nuns are married and have children. Most reside in the New York metropolitan area. One major B-WAC principal lives near the Canadian border.

8. Excerpted from A. Kahn, *Theory and Practice of Social Planning* (New York: Russell Sage Foundation, 1969).

9. In June 1985, James Farmer called for a national coalition think tank for program or plan development and formulation of strategies for social change.

10. Ms. Delta discussed these issues during the author's fall 1982 interview in Brooklyn, New York.

11. From the author's interviews with the leader-client Joyce Burson during the summer of 1983.

12. Ibid.

Bibliography

Alinsky, Saul. *Reveille for Radicals*. New York: Vintage Books, 1969.

Anderson, Elijah. *A Place on the Corner*. Chicago: University of Chicago Press, 1975.

Ash, Roberta. *Social Movements in America*. Chicago: Markham, 1972.

Bailis, Laurence. *Break of Justice: Grass Roots Organizing in the Welfare Rights Movement*. Lexington, Mass.: Heath, 1974.

Becker, Selwyn, and Duncan Neuhauser. *The Efficient Organization*. New York: Elsevier Scientific Publishers, 1975.

Bedford-Stuyvesant-New York Reporter. January–December 1969.

Beecham, Nannette. "Your Picture to Combat Organized Crime." *Welfare Righter*, March 28, 1969.

Bender, Thomas. *Community and Social Change*. New Brunswick, N.J.: Rutgers University Press, 1978.

Bennett, Lerone Jr. *Confrontation: Black and White*. Baltimore: Penguin Books, 1968.

Berger, Peter, and Richard Neuhaus. *To Empower People: The Role of Mediating Structures in Public Policy*. *American Enterprise*. Washington, D.C.: Institute for Public Policy Research, 1977.

Blau, Paul. *Exchange and Power in Social Life*. New York: Wiley, 1964.

Blumer, Herbert. In *Social Movements: Principles of Sociology*, edited by Alfred M. Lee. New York: Barnes and Noble, 1962, pp. 199–220.

_____. "Social Problems as Collective Behavior." *Social Problems* 8 (1971): 298–305.

Bremner, Robert. *From the Depths: The Discovery of Poverty in the United States*. New York: New York University Press, 1956.

Cade, Toni. *The Black Woman: An Anthology*. New York : Signet Press, 1970.

Cameron, William Bruce. *Modern Social Movements: A Sociological Outline*. New York: Random House, 1966.

Cantarow, Ellen. *Moving the Mountain: Women Working for Social Change*. New York: Feminist Press / McGraw-Hill, 1980.

Castells, Manuel. *The City and the Grass Roots*. Berkeley: University of California Press, 1983.

Charon, Joel M. *The Meaning of Sociology: A Reader*. Sherman Oaks, Calif.: Alfred Publishing, 1981.

Clark, Kenneth B. *Dark Ghetto: Dilemmas of Social Power*. New York: Harper and Row, 1967.

Cloward, Richard, and Frances Fox Piven. *The Politics of Turmoil: Poverty, Race and the Urban Crisis*. New York: Vintage Books, 1973.

_____. *Poor People's Movements: Why They Succeed, How They Fail*. New York: Vintage Books, 1979.

_____. *Regulating the Poor: The Functions of Public Welfare*. New York: Vintage Books, 1971.

_____. "A Strategy to End Poverty." *Nation*. May 2, 1966.

Coles, Robert, and Jane Hallowell. *Women of Crises. Lives of Struggle and Hope*. New York: Dell Publishing, 1979.

Coser, Lewis. *The Functions of Social Conflict*. New York: Free Press, 1956.

Covian, Sherrell. "Steps to Control Welfare Centers." *Welfare Righter*, March 28, 1969.

"Cracks in the Big Rock Candy Mountain." New York *Daily News*. September 15, 1968.

Cummings, Bernice, and Victoria Schuck. *Women Organizing: An Anthology*. Metuchen, N.J.: Scarecrow Press, 1979.

Currie, Elliot, and Jerome Skolnick. *A Critical Note on Conceptions of Collective Bargaining: Crisis in American Institutions*. Boston, Mass.: Little, Brown, 1970.

Davis, Angela Y. "Reflections on the Black Women's Role in the Community of Slaves." *Black Scholar* 3, 4 (1971): 69–79.

_____. *Women, Race and Class*. New York: Random House, 1981.

De Tocqueville, Alexis. *Democracy in America*. New York: Vintage Books, 1957.

Dumhoff, G. William. *Who Rules America?* Englewood Cliffs, N.J.: Spectrum Books, 1967.

Durbin, Elizabeth. *Welfare Income and Employment—An Economic Analysis of Family Choice*. New York: Praeger Publishers, 1969.

Dworkin, Andrea. *Right Wing Women*. New York: Putnam, 1983.

Etzioni, Amitai. *Social Change: Sources, Patterns and Consequences*. New York: Basic Books, 1964.

_____. *Social Problems*. Englewood Cliffs, N.J.: Prentice-Hall, 1976.

_____. *Studies in Social Change*. New York: Holt, Rhinehart, and Winston, 1961.

Fainstein, Norman, and Susan Fainstein. *Urban Political Movements.* Englewood Cliffs, N.J.: Prentice-Hall, 1974.

_____. *The View from Below Urban: Politics and Social Policy* (anthology). Boston, Mass.: Little, Brown, 1972.

Faludi, Andreas. *Planning Theory.* New York: Pergamon Press, 1973.

_____. *A Reader in Planning Theory.* New York: Pergamon Press, 1973.

Feagin, Joe. *Subordinating the Poor: Welfare and American Beliefs.* Englewood Cliffs, N.J.: Prentice-Hall, 1975.

"Federal Guidelines for Increased Income." *Welfare Righter.* June 27, 1969.

Ferman, Louise, Joyce Kornbluh, and Alan Haber. *Poverty in America* (a book of readings). Ann Arbor: University of Michigan Press, 1965.

Flatbush Life. January–August 1969.

Froland, Charles, et al. *Helping Networks and Human Services.* Beverly Hills, Calif.: Sage Publications, 1981.

Gamson, William A. *The Strategy of Social Protest.* Homewood, Ill.: Dorsey Press, 1975.

_____. *People and Plans: Essays on Urban Problems and Solutions.* New York: Basic Books, 1968.

_____. "Uses of Poverty: The Poor Pay All." In *The Meaning of Sociology: A Reader,* edited by Joel Charon. Sherman Oaks, Calif.: Alfred Publishing, 1980, pp. 348–415.

Garner, Roberta Ash. *Social Change.* Chicago: Rand McNally, 1977.

Gittell, Marilyn, and Nancy Naples. "Women Activists and Community Organization." In *Report to the Carnegie Foundation.* New York: CUNY Press, November 1981, pp. 1–54.

Gittell, Marilyn, and Theresa Shtob. "Changing Women's Roles in Political Volunteerism and Reform of the City." *Signs: Journal of Women in Culture and Society* 5, 3 (1980): 67–68.

Glazer, Barney G., and Anselm L. Strass. *The Discovery of Grounded Theory: Strategies for Qualitative Research.* Chicago: Aldine Publishing, 1967.

Glazer, William (editor). *The Government of Associations: Selections from the Behavioral Sciences.* Totowa, N.J.: Bedminister Press, 1966.

Goodman, Robert. *After the Planners.* Beaverton, Oreg.: Touchstone, 1971.

Goodwin, Leonard. *Do the Poor Want to Work? A Socio-Psychological Study of Work Orientations.* Washington, D.C.: Brookings Institute, 1972.

Gordon, Suzanne. *Lonely in America.* New York: Simon and Schuster, 1976.

Gornick, Vivian, and Barbara Moran. *Women in a Sexist Society.* New York: Mentor Books, 1971.

Gottlieb, Naomi. *The Welfare Bind.* New York: Columbia University Press, 1974.

Gross, Bertram. *Friendly Fascism: The New Face of America.* Boston, Mass.: South End Press, 1980.

Grosser, Charles. *New Directions in Community Organizations: From Ena-*

bling to Advocacy. New York: Praeger Publishers, 1973.

Guttentag, Marcia. "Group Cohesiveness: Ethnic Organization and Poverty." *Journal of Social Issues* 26, 2 (Spring 1970).

Hall, Richard, and Robert Quinn (editors). *Organizational Theory and Public Policy*. Sage Publications, 1983.

Harrington, Michael. *The Other America: Poverty in the U.S.* Baltimore: Penguin Books, 1963.

Hartman, John, and Jack Hedblom. *Methods for the Social Sciences: A Handbook for Students and Non-Specialists*. Westport, Conn.: Greenwood Press, 1979.

Harward, Donald (editor). *Power: Its Nature, Its Use, and Its Limits*. Cambridge, Mass.: Schenkman Publishing, 1979.

Hertz, Susan. "The Politics of the Welfare Mothers' Movement: A Case Study." *Signs: Journal of Women in Culture and Society* 2, 3 (Spring 1977).

Higginbotham, Elizabeth. "Educated Black Women: An Exploration into Life Chances and Choices." Doctoral dissertation, Brandeis University, Sociology Department, 1970.

Hirsch, Eric. "The Creation of Political Solidarity in Social Movement Organizations "*Sociological Quarterly* 27, no. 3 (1986).

Hochman, Harold. *The Urban Economy*. New York: Norton, 1976.

Hood, Elizabeth. "Black Women, White Women: Separate Paths to Liberation." *Black Scholar* 14 (September–October 1983): 26–37. Reprint.

Howe, Irving, and Michael Harrington. *The Seventies: Problems and Proposals*. New York: Harper and Row, 1972.

Hylan, John, and James Regan. "Poverty Movement: Medieval Europe and Brooklyn 1960–1970." Unpublished report, 1979.

Jackson, Larry, and William Johnson. *Protest by the Poor: The Welfare Rights Movement in New York City*. New York: Rand Corporation, 1968.

Jenkins, Craig J. "Resource Mobilization Theory and the Study of Social Movements." *Annual Review of Sociology* (1983): 527–53.

Kahn, Alfred J. *Studies in Social Policy and Planning*. New York: Russell Sage Foundation, 1969.

_____. *Theory and Practice of Social Planning*. New York: Russell Sage Foundation, 1969.

Katz, Michael. *Poverty and Policy in American History: Studies in Social Discontinuity*. Orlando, Fl.: Academic, 1983.

KNIC-NAC, The Voice of the Poor. September 25, 1967; December 25, 1967; April 30, 1968; January 6, 1969.

Komisar, Lucy. *Down and Out in the USA: A History of Social Welfare*. New Viewpoints, 1974.

Kotz, Nickolas. *A Passion for Equality*. New York: Norton, 1976.

Kramer, Ralph, and Harry Specht. *Readings in Community Organization Practice*. Englewood Cliffs, N.J.: Prentice-Hall, 1969.

Ladner, Joyce. *Tomorrow's Tomorrows: The Black Woman*. New York: Doubleday Anchor Books, 1971.

Lauffer, Armand. *Social Planning at the Community Level*. Englewood Cliffs, N.J.: Prentice-Hall, 1978.

Leavitt, Jacqueline. "Research Needs and Guidelines on Women's Issues: Planning, Housing and Community Development." *Columbia University Papers in Planning #17*, New York, 1980.

Lerner, Gerda. *Black Women in White America: A Documentary History*. New York: Vintage Books, 1973.

Levitan, Sar. *Programs in Aid of the Poor*. Baltimore, Md.: Johns Hopkins University Press, 1976.

Lewis, Diane K. "A Response to Inequality: Black Women, Racism and Sexism." *Signs: Journal of Women in Culture and Society* 3, 2 (Winter 1977).

Lipsky, Michael. *Street-Level Bureaucracy*. New York: Russell Sage Foundation, 1980.

Mandell, Betty R. (editor). *Welfare in America: Controlling the Dangerous Classes. The Handout as a Form of Social Control*. Englewood Cliffs, N.J.: Spectrum Books, 1975.

Marcuse, Herbert. *One-Dimensional Man*. Boston, Mass.: Beacon Press, 1964.

Marx, Gary and Michael Useem. "Majority Involvement in Minority Movements." *Journal of Social Issues* 27, 1 (1971).

Matoni, Charles. "The Priests of '63." *Newsday Magazine*, November 27, 1983, pp. 8–30.

Mayer, Robert. *Social Planning and Social Change*. Englewood Cliffs, N.J.: Prentice-Hall, 1971.

Mayo, Judith. *Work and Welfare: Employment and Employability of Women in the AFDC Program*. University of Chicago, Center for Community and Family Study, 1975.

McCarthy, John D., and Mayer N. Zald. "Resource Mobilization and Social Movements: A Partial Theory" *American Journal of Sociology* 82 (May 1977): 1212–41.

Meadows, Paul. *The Many Faces of Change*. Cambridge, Mass.: Schenkman Publishing, 1971.

Meenaghan, Thomas, and Robert Washington. *Social Policy and Social Welfare: Structure and Applications*. New York: Free Press, 1980.

Meier, August, and Elliott Rudwick. *From Plantation to Ghetto*. New York: Hill and Wang Press, 1976.

Merton, Robert K. *Social Theory and Social Structure*. Glencoe, Ill.: Free Press, 1957.

Milwaukee County Welfare Rights Organization. *We Ain't Gonna Shuffle Anymore*. Norton Press, 1972.

Mills, C. Wright. *The Sociological Imagination*. New York: Grove Press, 1961.

Moynihan, Daniel. *Toward a National Urban Policy*. New York: Basic Books, 1961.

Newfield, Jack and Paul DuBrul. *The Abuse of Power: The Permanent Government and the Fall of New York.* New York: Penguin Books, 1978.

Newman, Dorothy, et al. *Protest, Politics and Prosperity: Black Americans and White Institutions, 1940–75.* New York: Pantheon Books, 1978.

New York City Commission on Human Rights. *Women's Role in Contemporary Society.* New York: Avon, 1972.

New York City Department of City Planning. Data compiled from the U.S. Department of Commerce, Bureau of the Census, 1970.

New York City Department of Welfare. *Monthly Statistical Reports.* June, July, and August 1963, 1966, and 1968; January 1966 and 1969.

New York City, *Monthly Statistical Reports.* 1966, 1967, and 1969; June, July, and August 1963 and 1968.

New York *Daily News.* July 3 and 4, 1968; August 27, 28, 29, 30, and 31, 1968; April 16, 1969.

New York *Post.* August 14, 27, 29, 1968.

New York *Reporter.* Editorial, November 15, 1969.

New York State Department of Social Service, Bureau of Data Management and Analysis. "Milestones in Public Welfare in New York State 1626–1978," Program brief #2, September 1979.

New York *Times.* July 2, 3, and 15, 1968; August 14, 15, 16, 23, 27, 28, and 29, 1968; July 20, 1969.

NOW. The National Welfare Leaders Newsletter. October and December 1968.

Oberschall, Anthony. *Social Conflict and Social Movements.* Englewood Cliffs, N.J.: Prentice-Hall, 1973.

Olson, Mancur Jr. *The Logic of Collective Action: Public Goods and the Theory of Groups.* Cambridge, Mass.: Harvard University Press, 1965.

Perry, Ronald. *Social Movements and the Local Community.* Beverly Hills, Calif.: Sage Publications, 1976.

Pierson, Frank C. *Community Manpower Services for the Disadvantaged.* Kalamazoo: Upjohn Institute for Employment Research, 1972.

Piven, Frances Fox, and Richard Cloward. *The New Class War: Reagan's Attacks on the Welfare State and Its Consequences.* New York: Random House, Pantheon Books, 1982.

Plant, Raymond. *Community and Ideology: An Essay in Applied Social Philosophy.* Boston, Mass.: Routledge and Kegan Paul, 1974.

Pope, Jacqueline. "Welfare Means to Go Well." *Concern Magazine* (November 1971): 9–10.

"Reform Measure Draws Fire from Black Rights Experts." *Jet.* August 28, 1969.

Reiss, Ira. *Family System in America.* New York: Holt, Rhinehart, and Winston, 1971.

Reitano, Joanne. "Working Girls Unite." *American Quarterly* 36 (Spring 1984): 112–34.

Roberts, Helen. *Doing Feminist Research*. Boston: Routledge and Kegan Paul, 1981.

Ross, Heather, and Isabel Sawhill. *Time of Transition: The Growth of Families Headed by Women*. Washington, D.C.: Urban Institute, 1975.

Ross, Murray. *Community Organization*. New York: Harper and Row, 1955.

Rothman, David. *The Discovery of the Asylum*. Boston, Mass.: Little, Brown, 1971.

Rothschild, Constantina. *Women and Social Policy*. Englewood Cliffs, N.J.: Prentice-Hall, 1974.

Rushing, William, and Mayer Zald (editors). *Organizations and Beyond. Selected Essays of James D. Thompson*. Lexington, Mass.: Lexington Books, 1976.

Ryan, William. *Blaming the Victim*. New York: Vintage Books, 1971; revised 1976.

Sampson, Timothy. *Welfare: A Handbook for Friend or Foe*. New York: Pilgrim Press, 1973.

Schorr, Alvin L. *Explorations in Social Policy*. New York: Basic Books, 1968.

Sclar, Elliott. "Social Cost Minimization: A National Policy Approach to the Problems of Distressed Economic Regions." In *The Zero Sum Society*, edited by Lester Thurow. New York: Basic Books, 1980.

Scott, David. *Don't Mourn For Me, Organize: The Social and Political Uses of Voluntary Organizations*. Winchester, Mass.: Allen and Unwin, 1981.

Scott, Richard. *Organizations: Rational, Natural and Open Systems*. Englewood Cliffs, N.J.: Prentice-Hall, 1981.

Segalman, Ralph, and Asoke Basu. *Poverty in America*. Westport, Conn.: Greenwood Press, 1981.

Selznick, Philip. *TVA and the Grass Roots*. New York: Harper and Row, 1966.

Sheehan, Susan. *A Welfare Mother*. Boston, Mass.: Houghton Mifflin, 1976.

Silberman, Charles. "Revolt against Welfare Colonialism." In *Crisis in Black and White*. New York: Basic Books, 1964.

Smelser, Neil. *Theory of Collective Behavior*. New York: Free Press, 1962.

Smith, Thelma. *Guide to the Municipal Government of the City of New York*. New York: Meilan Press, 1973.

Sparer, Edward V. "The Illegality of Poverty." *Journal of Social Policy* (March–April 1971): 49–53.

Spergel, Irving (editor). *Community Organization: Studies in Constraint*. Beverly Hills, Calif.: Sage Publications, 1972.

"Spring Clothing Drive Hits Welfare Department." *KNIC-NAC, The Voice of the Poor*. April 30, 1968.

Stack, Carol B. *All Our Kin: Strategies for Survival in a Black Community*. New York: Harper and Row, Colophon Books, 1974.

Staples, Robert. *The Black Woman in America*. Chicago: Nelson-Hall, 1973.

Steiner, Gilbert. *Social Insecurity: The Politics of Welfare*. Chicago: Rand McNally, 1966.

Stevens, John, and George Matthews. "The Church in Bedford Stuyvesant." Proposal submitted to the Brooklyn Catholic diocese, 1967.

"Stores to Open Credit to NWRO Members." *Welfare Righter*. March 28, 1969.

Street, David, George Martin, and Laura Kramer Gordon. *The Welfare Industry: Functionaries and Recipients in Public Aid*. Beverly Hills, Calif.: Sage Publications, 1979.

Tablet, The. Roman Catholic weekly. March 3, 21, and 28, 1968; April 4, 11, 25, and 28, 1968; May 2, 1968; July 14 and 16, 1968.

Tillman, Johnnie. "Insights of a Welfare Mother." *Journal of Social Issues* (January–February 1971): 13–23. Reprint.

Tilly, Charles. *Social Movements and National Politics*. College Park, Md.: University of Maryland Press, 1979.

Titmus, Richard M. *Commitment to Welfare*. New York: Random House, Pantheon Books, 1968.

_____. *The Gift Relationship*. Winchester, Mass.: Allen and Unwin, 1970.

_____. *Social Policy*. New York: Random House, Pantheon Books, 1974.

Trattner, Walter. *From Poor Law to Welfare State: A History of Social Welfare in America*. New York: Free Press, 1974.

Tullock, Gordon. *Private Wants, Public Means: An Economic Analysis of the Desirable Scope of Government*. New York: Basic Books.

U.S. Department of Commerce, Bureau of the Census. *Historical Statistics of the United States, Colonial Times to 1970*, Vol. 2. Washington, D.C.: Government Printing Office, 1975.

_____. *Income Characteristics of the Population: 1970*. Washington, D.C.: Government Printing Office, 1970.

U.S. Department of Labor, Employment and Training Division, Bureau of Labor Statistics. *Regional Manpower Administration Notice #1-72*. Press release. March 17, 1969.

Useem, Michael. *Protest Movements in America*. New York: Bobbs-Merrill, 1975.

Valentine, Betty Lou. *Hustling and Other Hard Work*. New York: Free Press, 1975.

Valentine, Charles A. *Culture and Poverty*. Chicago: University of Chicago Press, 1968.

Weber, Max. *The Protestant Ethic and the Spirit of Capitalism*. New York: Charles Scribner's Sons, 1958.

"Welfare: Trying to End the Nightmare." *Time*. February 8, 1971, pp. 14–23.

Welfare Fighter. January–December 1970; August 1971; August–October 1972.

Welfarer, The. January–February 1966.

Welfare Righter. June 1968.

Wellstone, Paul. *How the Rural Poor Got Power: Narrative of a Grassroots Organizer.* Amherst, Mass.: University of Massachusetts Press, 1978.

West, Guida. *The National Welfare Rights Movement — The Social Protest of Poor Women.* New York: Praeger Publishers, 1981.

Wiebe, Robert. *The Search for Order.* Westport, Conn.: Greenwood Press.

Williams, James (editor). *The State of Black America 1979.* Washington, D.C.: National Urban League, 1979.

Wilson, William Julius. *The Declining Significance of Race: Blacks and Changing American Institutions.* Chicago: University of Chicago Press, 1978.

Wright, Gwendolyn. *Building the Dream.* New York: Random House, Pantheon Books, 1971.

Zald, Mayer, and Roberta Ash. "Social Movement Organizations: Growth, Decay and Change." *Social Forces* 44 (March 1966).

Zaretsky, Eli. *Capitalism, The Family and Personal Life.* New York: Harper and Row, Colophon Books, 1973.

Index

ABOUT THE AUTHOR

JACQUELINE POPE is an assistant professor of political science at Stockton State College in Pomona, New Jersey, with a Ph.D. from Columbia University. She specializes in public administration and policy and urban studies. Teaching is a career change for her, having spent 20 years in public-policy change advocacy for the poor and in research with nonprofit organizations, including the New York City government.

This first book documents activities of the Brooklyn Welfare Action Council, whose members were society's poorest women. They labored virtually alone to promote equity for their children and themselves. "Many of us believe it heralded the true beginning of the women's movement in New York City," according to Dr. Pope.